PERTH ASSEMBLY

CONTAINING

1. The Proceedings thereof.
2. The Proof of the Nullity thereof.
3. Reasons presented thereto against the receiving the five new *Articles* imposed.
4. The oppositeness of it to the proceedings and oath of the whole state of the Land. *Anno* 1581.
5. Proofs of the unlawfulness of the said five Articles, *viz.* 1. Kneeling in the act of Receiving the Lord's Supper. 2. Holy days. 3. Bishopping. 4. Private Baptism. 5. Private Communion.

EXODUS 20:7
Thou shalt not take the name of the Lord thy God in vain, for the Lord will not hold him guiltless that taketh his name in vain.

COLOSSIANS 2:8
Beware lest there be any that spoil you through Philosophy & vain deceit, through the traditions of men, according to the rudiments of the World, and not of Christ.

MDCXIX

Puritan Reprints
www.puritanreprints.com
Edited by Greg Fox
Copyright © 2006 by Puritan Reprints
First Edition, 2006
ISBN-13: 978-0-9792165-4-1
ISBN-10: 0-9792165-4-0

CONTENTS

Editor's Preface vii

Biographical introduction of the author
taken from John Howie's *The Scots Worthies* ix

To the Reader 1

The Proceedings of the Assembly
Holden at Perth 5

The Nullity of Perth Assembly 19

The Articles Presented to the Assembly 29

The Oath Discussed 37

Kneeling in the Act of Receiving the Sacrament 47

Reasons Against Festival Days 87

Of Confirmation 119

Of Bishoping 127

Of the Administration of the Sacraments
in private places 133

Editor's Preface

Perth Assembly was written by David Calderwood in 1619. It was printed in Leyden, Holland by the Pilgrims just a year before they made the voyage to America to settle at Plymouth Colony. The book enraged King James I, who sent authorities to Holland to arrest William Brewster, the printer. Brewster fled to England and went into hiding. He was never apprehended, and later made the voyage to America in 1620.

Calderwood wrote *Perth Assembly* out of protest to King James' imposition of the "Five Articles" upon the Church of Scotland. He fled to Holland after publishing the book, and didn't return to Scotland until after the death of James I, in 1625.

This edition of *Perth Assembly* has had minor punctuation changes. The spelling has been corrected or updated to modern spelling in several places. The Elizabethan English is still intact despite the spelling corrections. All editorial additions, such as definitions of archaic words, are contained in brackets.

Greg Fox
January 25, 2007

David Calderwood
By John Howie

David Calderwood, having spent some time at the grammar-school, went to the university to study theology, in order for the ministry. After a short space, being found fit for that office, he was made minister of Crailing, near Jedburgh, where for some considerable time he preached the word of God with great wisdom, zeal, and diligence, and as a faithful wise husbandman brought in many sheaves into God's granary. But it being then a time when prelacy was upon the advance in the Church, and faithful ministers were everywhere thrust out and suppressed, he, among the rest, gave in his declinature in the year 1608, and thereupon took instruments in the hands of James Johnston, notary-public, in presence of some of the magistrates and council of the town. Whereupon, information being sent to King James VI [of Scotland, James I of England] by the bishops, a direction was sent down to the council to punish him, and another minister who declined, exemplarily. But by the earnest dealing of the Earl of Lothian with the Chancellor in favor of Mr. Calderwood, their punishment resolved itself only into confinement within their own parishes.

Here he continued until June 1617, when he was summoned to appear before the High Commission Court at St Andrews, upon the 8th of July following. Being called upon (the King being present), and his libel read and answered, the King, among other things, said, "What moved you to protest?" "An article concluded among the Lords of the Articles," Mr. Calderwood answered. "But what fault was there in it?" said the King. "It cutteth off our General Assemblies," he answered. The King, having the protestation in his hand, challenged him for some words of the last clause thereof. He answered, that whatsoever was the phrase of speech, it meant no other thing but to protest that they would give passive obedience to his Majesty, but could not give active obedience unto any unlawful thing which should flow from that article. "Active and passive obedience?" said the King. "That is, we will rather suffer than practice," said Calderwood. "I will tell thee," said the King, "what is obedience, man; what the centurion said to his servant, To this man, Go, and he goeth, and to that man, Come, and he cometh; that is obedience." He answered, "To suffer, Sire, is also obedience, howbeit not of the same kind; and that obedience was not absolute, but limited, with the exception of a countermand from a superior power." "I am informed," said the King, "ye are a refractor; the Archbishop of Glasgow your ordinary, the Bishop of Caithness, the Moderator, and your presbytery, testify ye have kept no order; ye have repaired to neither presbytery nor synod, and are no way conform." He answered, "I have been confined these eight or nine years, so my conformity or nonconformity in that point could not well be known." "Gude [good] faith! Thou art a very knave," said the King. "See these same false puritans, they are ever playing with equivocations." The King asked, whether, if he was released, he would obey or not? He answered, "I am wronged in that I am forced to answer such questions, which are beside the libel;" after which he was removed.

When called in again, it was intimated to him, that if he did not repair to synods and presbyteries between this and October, conform during that time, and promise obedience in all time coming, the Archbishop of Glasgow was to deprive him. Then Calderwood begged leave to speak to the bishops; which being granted, he reasoned thus: "Neither can ye suspend or deprive me in this Court of High Commission, for ye have no power in this court but by commission from his Majesty; and his Majesty cannot communicate that power to you which he claims not to himself." At this the King wagged his head, and said to him, "Are there not bishops and fathers in the church, persons clothed with power and authority to suspend and depose?" "Not in this court," answered Calderwood; at which words there arose a confused noise, so that he was obliged to extend his voice, that he might be heard. In the end the King asked him, if he would obey the sentence? To which he answered, "Your sentence is not the sentence of the Kirk, but a sentence null in itself, and therefore I cannot obey it." At this some, reviling, called him a proud knave; others were not ashamed to shake his shoulders, in a most insolent manner, till at last he was removed a second time.

Being again called in, the sentence of deprivation was pronounced, and he was ordained to be committed to close ward in the tolbooth [prison] of St. Andrews, till farther orders were taken for his banishment; after which he was upbraided by the Archbishop, who said that he deserved to be used as Ogilvy the Jesuit, who was hanged. When he would have answered, the bishops would not allow him, and the King, in a rage, cried, "Away with him;" and Lord Scone, taking him by the arm, led him out, where they stayed some time waiting for the bailiffs of the town.

In the meantime, Calderwood said to Scone, "My lord, this is not the first like turn that hath fallen into your hands." "I must serve the King," said Scone. To some ministers then standing by, Calderwood said, "Brethren, ye have Christ's cause in hand at this meeting; be not terrified with this spectacle, prove faithful servants to your Master." Scone took him to his house till the keys of the tolbooth were had. By the way, one demanded, "whither with the man, my lord?" "First to the tolbooth, and then to the gallows," said Scone.

He was committed close prisoner, and the same afternoon a charge was given to transport him to the jail of Edinburgh. After the charge, he was delivered to two of the guard to be transported thither; although several offered to bail him, that he might not go out of the country. But no order of Council could be had for that end; for the King had a design to keep him in close ward till a ship was ready to convey him first to London, and then to Virginia. But Providence had ordered otherwise; for, upon several petitions in his behalf, he was liberated from prison, Lord Cranston being bail that he should depart out of the country.

After this, Calderwood went with Lord Cranston to the King at Carlisle, where the said Lord presented a petition to him, that Mr. David might only be confined to his parish; but the King inveighed against him so much, that at last he repulsed Cranston with his elbow. He insisted again for a prorogation of time for his departure till the last of April, because of the winter-session, that he might have leisure to get up his year's stipend. The King answered, that however he begged, it were no matter; he would know himself better the next time; and, for the season of the year, if he drowned in the seas, he might thank God that he had escaped a worse death. Yet Cranston being so importunate for the prorogation, the King answered, "I will advise with my bishops." Thus the time was delayed until the year 1619, that he wrote a book, called "Perth Assembly," which was condemned by the Council in December that same year; but, as he himself says, neither the book nor the author could be found, for in August preceding he had embarked for Holland.

During his abode there, Patrick Scot, a landed gentleman near Falkland, having wasted his patrimony, had no other means to recover his estate, but by some unlawful shift at Court; and for that end, in the year 1624, he set forth a recantation, under the name of David Calderwood, who, because of his long sickness before, was supposed by many to have been dead. The King (as Scot alleged to some of his friends), furnished him with the matter, and he set it down in form. This project failing, Scot went over to Holland, in November, and sought Calderwood in several towns, particularly in Amsterdam, in order to dispatch him, as afterwards appeared. After he had stayed twenty days in Amsterdam, making all the search he could, he was informed that Calderwood had returned home privately to his native country, which frustrated his intention. After the death of King James, Scot published a pamphlet full of this, entitled *Vox vera*; and yet, notwithstanding of all his wicked and unlawful pursuits, he died soon after, so poor that he left not wherewith to defray the charges of his funeral.

David Calderwood being now returned home, after the death of King James VI, remained as private as possible, and was mostly at Edinburgh, where he strengthened the hands of nonconformists, being also a great opposer of sectarianism, until after the year 1638, when he was admitted minister of Pencaitland, in East Lothian.

He contributed very much to the covenanted work carried on in that period. For first he had an active hand in drawing up several excellent papers, wherein were contained the records of church-policy betwixt the year 1576 and 1596, which were presented and read by Mr. Johnston, the clerk, at the General Assembly at Glasgow, in 1638. He was also, by recommendation of the General Assembly 1646, required to consider the order of the visitation of kirks, and trials of Presbyteries, and to make report thereof unto the next General Assembly; and likewise, at the General Assembly 1648, a further recommendation was given to him, to make a draft of the form of visitation of particular congregations, against the next Assembly. He was also one of those appointed, with Mr. David Dickson, to draw up the form of the Directory for the public worship of God, by the General Assembly 1643.

After he had both spent and been spent, with the apostle, for the cause and interest of Jesus Christ, when the English army lay at Lothian in 1651, he went to Jedburgh, where he sickened, and died in a good old age. He was another valiant champion for the truth, who, in pleading for the crown and interest of Jesus Christ, knew not what it was to be daunted by the face and frowns of the highest and most incensed adversaries.

xiv

Before he went to Holland, he wrote the book entitled, "Perth Assembly." While in Holland, he wrote that learned book called *Altare Damascenum*, with some other pieces in English, which contributed somewhat to keep many straight in that declining period. After his return, he wrote the history of our Church as far down as the year 1625; of which, the printed copy that we have is only a short abstract of that large written history, which both as to the style and the manner wherein it is executed, is far preferable to the printed copy. Whoever compares the two, or the last, with his *Altare Damascenum* – both of which are yet in the hands of some – will readily grant the truth of this assertion; and yet all this derogates nothing from the truth of the facts reported in the printed copy; and therefore, no offence need be taken at the information, that there is a more full and better copy than has yet been printed.[1]

"The Wood is fallin, the Church not built,
Nor Reformation endit;
The Cedar great is now cutt doun,
Who first that Work intendit.

"By toung and pen he did not fear
T' oppose proud Prelacie;
His Scriptural arguments did prevail
Against their Hierarchie.

"Both Sectaries and Schismaticks
He did convince with reasoun;
His Lyff and Papers weil record
He did abhor their treasoun,

---

[1] This better copy, which is here referred to, has since been published by the Wodrow Society in seven volumes. These form an interesting memorial of him whom Baillie describes as "that living magazine of our ecclesiastical history, most Reverend Master Calderwood." From the valuable appendix contained in the eighth volume, we borrow the following elegy on his death. – Ed. [W. H. Carslaw, D.D.]

"Sing hymnes of joy, sweit soul, in peace,
    Unto thy great Redeemer;
    Untill this persecuted clay
    Be joyn'd with Thee for ever."

TO THE READER

The external worship of God, and the government of the Church (Gentle and judicious reader) are like Hippocrates twins: they are sick together, in health together: they live together, they die and dwine [waste away] together. As long as the government of the Church of Scotland stood in integrity, as it was established by laws, civil and ecclesiastical, according to God's word, so long was the worship of God preserved in purity. Since the former government was altered, and the insolent domination of Prelates hath entered in by unlawful means amongst us; popish rites and superstitious Ceremonies have followed, and are like to prevail universally. They have verified in their persons their common tenet, No Ceremony, no Bishop. The liberty granted to our Church, to indict and hold general assemblies from year to year and oftener *pro re nata*, was the chief bulwark of our discipline. This bulwark was broken down to the end a more patent way might be made for their exaltation. When vote in Parliament (the needle to draw in the thread of Episcopal authority) was concluded, to the great grief of the sincerer sort, many protestations were made, that no alteration in discipline, or divine service was intended: many cautions and limitations were made to bound the power of the minister voter in Parliament. They were ordained to be countable to the general Assemblies, for the manner of their entry and behavior in this new office: But like bankrupts, not being able to render account, they labored that no account should be made at all: that is, that there should be no ordinary general assembly to take account. Some few extraordinary Assemblies have been convocated of late years at their pleasures, for their purposes, and according to their device, constituted as they thought good: wherein they procured, or rather extorted with terror and authority, a sort of preeminence above their brethren. They were Lords in Parliament, Council, Session, Checker, Lords of Regalities, Lords of temporal lands, Presenters to benefices, modifiers of Minister's stipends, grand-Commissioners in the high Commission. Was it wonder then if so great Commanders commanded the Assemblies constituted, as is said, and carved to themselves a spiritual Lordship, when their worthy brethren were banished, imprisoned, confined, or detained at Court, that they might the more easily effectuate their purpose. They have broken the caveats made with their own consent, violated their promises, and have sought preeminence both in Church and Common- wealth, with the ruin of others, and the renting of their mothers belly. We have notwithstanding been so silent hitherto, that the world hath judged our silence, rather slumbering and slothfulness then true patience. They are not satisfied with the wrongs already committed, but do still provoke us with new irritant occasions: and specially by obtruding upon us superstitious will-worships, and polluted inventions of men. It behooveth us therefore to set pen to paper, and say somewhat for the surer stay and better information of professors, tenderly affected to the sincerity of religion, lest they be deluded with the glorious name of a pretended and null-Assembly, or seduced with temporizers, swallowing up all abominations or corruptions whatsoever. The means of printing and publishing are to us very difficult: we wish therefore every good Christian to take in good part our mean travels, and not impute unto us want of good will, but of means, if they be not served hereafter continually after this manner. We shall be ready God willing for our own part, as need shall require, and opportunity will serve, to defend the cause we maintain against any of our opposites their answers, or replies whatsoever, worthy of answer. We have seen of late some Pamphlets, which have rather exposed their authors to laughter and contempt, then deserved any serious

Confutation. In the Epistle before Basilikon Doron his Majesty protesteth upon his honor, that he misliketh not generally all Preachers, or others, who like better of the single form of Policy in our Church, then of the many Ceremonies in the Church of England: and are persuaded that their Bishops smell of a papal Supremacy, that the surplesse [vestment], the corner cap, and such like, are the outward badges of popish errors, and that he doth equally love and honor the learned and grave men of either of these opinions. His Majesty useth this Provision, that where the Law is otherwise, they press by Patience and well grounded reasons, either to persuade all the rest to like of their judgment, or where they see better grounds on the other part, not to be ashamed peaceably to incline thereunto, laying aside all preoccupied opinions. We are able to prove that no Ecclesiastical law hath been made in any free and formal Assembly for the alterations by-past, or presently intended, either in Government or Ceremonies. The ratification of civil Laws already made, or to be made, cannot rectify the Ecclesiastical, as long as we are able by good reason to impugn their authority, and evince the vicious constitution, the informal and unlawful proceedings of these Assemblies, where the said Ecclesiastical Laws are said to have been made. Put the case that no exception might be made against the Law, his Majesty's provision permitteth us to persuade others with well grounded reasons. The verity of our relations, and validity of our reasons, we refer to the trial of every judicious Reader, making conscience of his oath, promise, subscription, and purity of his profession.

THE PROCEEDINGS
OF THE ASSEMBLY HOLDEN
at PERTH in August, *Anno Dom.* 1618

Tuesday the 25th of August, 1618, the first day of the Assembly. The general Assembly was indicted by his Majesty to be holden at Perth the 25th day of August 1618. Intimation was made twenty days before by open proclamation with sound of trumpet. For obedience to the proclamation and his Majesty's particular missives, the persons following convened at the said Burgh the appointed day: his Majesty's Commissioners my Lord *Binning* Secretary, *Lord Skoone, Lord Carnegie*. Their Assessors *Sir Gideon Murray* Treasurer Deputy, *Sir Andrew Ker* of *Pharnihirst*, Captain of the guard. *Sir William Olphant* the king's Advocate, and *Sir Wil. Livingstoun* of *Kilsyth*. Noble men, the *Earls of Louthiane, Lord Ochiltrie, Lord Sanquhar, Lord Boyde*. Barons: *Waughtoun, Lutquharne, Glenvrquhart* younger, *Clunie-Gordoun, Boningtoun-woode, Weymis, Balvaird, Bilcolmie, Balcarras, Balmanno, Bombie, Blackbarronie, Lagg*. Burgesses: for *Edinburgh David Akinheid George Fowlis*. For *Perth James Aedie, Constant Malice*. For *Dundee; Mr. Alexander Wedderburne* younger, *Robert Clay-hils*: for *Aberdine, Mr. John Mortimer*. For *Sterling, Christopher Alexander*: for *St. Andrews, John Knox, Thomas Lentroun*: for the University of *St. Andrews, Doctor Bruce*. Bishops, all except *Argyle* and the Isles, Ministers, Commissioners from presbyteries.

According to the ordinance, and laudable custom of this Church anent the sanctification of her meetings by fasting and prayer, intimation was made upon the Sabbath preceding in the Church of Perth of a fast to be observed the first day of the assembly: but the fast was little regarded, saving that two sermons were made. The first was made in the morning by

Patrik Bishop of Aberdeen. His text, *Ezra 7:23* he observed and enlarged this ground, that nothing should be done or determined in the Church by any superior power whatsoever, but that which is according to the commandment of the almighty King. The other sermon was made at the tenth hour by John Archbishop of Saint Andrews in the little Church. His text, *1 Corinthians 11:16* was very pertinent, but he ran quickly from it. He discoursed the space of two hours first in defense of ceremonies in general. Next, of the five articles in particular. His best arguments for proof or improbation was some testimonies cited out of Calvin, Martyr, Beza, but perverted. The said Arch Bishop in his discourse, made ample protestation that he understood not of the intended novations before they came of his Majesty. Item, that his Majesty would have had these five Articles registered as Canons in the book of the general Assembly, without either reasoning or voting: but by his means his Majesty was put of, till the consent of the Church should be obtained. This his protestation he confirmed with a dreadful execration, that the curse of God might light on him, and his, if he had not spoken truly. Immediately after the said discourse; was holden the first Session of this assembly in manner following.

    There was set in the little Church a long table, and at the head thereof a short cross table. At the cross table were set chairs for his Majesty's Commissioners and the Moderator. At the side of the long table were set forms for Noblemen, Barons, Burgesses, Bishops and Doctors. The Ministers were left to stand behind them, as if their place and part had been only to behold.

    The Archbishop placed himself at the head of the table in the Moderators chair beside his Majesty's Commissioners. After prayer he notified to the assembly, that Master Thomas Nicolson ordinary Clark had demitted his office in favor of Master James Sandelands Advocate. He commended the said Master James, as a man qualified for that office, and ready to further the brethren in their particular affaires: And so without formal voting or lyte [nomination] he took him sworn and admitted him Clerk. The Brethren were ordained to give in their commissions to him after the rising of this session.

After that, Doctor Young, Dean of Winchester, by birth a Scotishman presented his Majesty's letter, directed to the Lords of the privy Counsel, and the Bishops. This letter was twice read in open audience. Terrors were mixed with allurements to move the assembly. After the reading of his Majesty's letter the Archbishop had a speech, wherein he protested, that neither he nor the Church of England had craved these novations, nor given counsel there anent, and that it was against his will, that ever they were motioned. Yet now he is persuaded, that his Majesty would be more glad of the consent of this assembly thereunto, then of all the gold of India: assuring them on the other part in case of their refusal, the whole estate and order of our Church will be overthrown, Some Ministers will be banished: other some will be deprived of their stipend and office; and all will be brought under the wrath of authority. He advised them rather to consent in time, then afterward to beg favor by offering conformity, and find none. He alleged a letter written to him by a banished minister, M. John Sharp, requesting liberty to serve God in his own country, and offering to submit himself in all things. But the letter was neither read nor seen. O, said he, I know when some of you are banished, and others deprived, ye will blame us, and call us persecutors; but we will lay all the burden upon the King. And if you call him a persecutor, all the world will stand up against you.

After his own speech, he required Doctor Young to speak, if so be, he had intention or commission to that effect. The Doctor after his preface of insinuation, laid out the proceedings of the last assembly holden at St. Andrews, the taunt and reproaches breathed out at Court against the same: his Majesty's high displeasure kindled by occasion thereof, like a flame of fire ready to consume all, except it were quenched in this present assembly by condescending to the five articles. He taxed the state of our Church, whereof he was ignorant. It pleased his wisdom to bring in the Puritan and the Papist, like Herod and Pilate conspiring *Si non contra Christum Deminum, tamen contra Christum Domini*. In end with words framed for the purpose and uttered in a mourning manner, he went about to catch consent to the five articles.

The minister's defenders of the established order perceiving the drift of these discourses, and all other means to be prepared and disposed for dashing of simple men, modestly required four things. 1. That none be admitted to vote, but such as are authorized with lawful commission. The Archbishop answered, his Majesty had written to noble men and Barons willing them to be present at this assembly, if any man had any exception against them, they should be heard. It was replied that they were not to except against their honorable persons or presence; but earnestly to crave that the order of the Church might be observed: whereby it is provided that without commission none have place to vote in general assemblies.

2. That the liberty of the Church be not broken in the election of the Moderator, and that a lawful lyte [nomination] be made to that effect. It was answered by the Archbishop that, this Assembly is convocate within the bounds of his diocese he would understand who will take his province over his head. So he intruded himself in the Moderators office without election.

3. That the articles proponed in short and general sums, might be put in form, and amply extended as his Majesty would have them enacted, that they may be the better advised and considered. The pretended Moderator answered, let alone these toys, trouble us not with needless questions, we shall speak of these things in the privy conference.

4. That some of either opinion may be set apart to collect, and put in order the reasons of either side for the more sure & easy information of the assemblies. The pretended moderator rejected this also as impertinent.

He proceeded at his own pleasure without advice or information of the provinces or presbyteries to the nomination of the privy conference, before that the Clark had received the commissions. He nominated besides his Majesty's commissioners, their assessors and the noble men, all the Barons except three, all the Bishops, the Commissioners of Edinburgh, Perth, Dundee, 37 Doctors and other ministers. The most part was such, as were already resolved to yield. Others were not experienced in the state of our Church, some few of the other opinion were taken in, to try the force of their arguments in private, that in public they might either be evaded, or suppressed. After the said nomination the conference was appointed to convene at 3 afternoon and the assembly at 8 hours in the morning. So endeth the first session.

The conference convened at 3 afternoon. His Majesty's letter was read again. The Moderator aforesaid seconded the same with many terrors. To make them go quickly to work, he affirmed that four articles were already concluded in the Assemblies holden last at Aberdeen and St. Andrews respective, howbeit not in form as his Majesty required: that kneeling allanerly [only] rested to be consented unto. For assisting of his declaration a minute was read containing the points conferred upon at the places foresaid. And no further evidence was produced for probation of the alleged agreement. But particularly mention was made, that his Highness altogether refused cautions and conditions added by the said Assemblies as frustrations of his Highness intentions. And as was affirmed by the said Moderator, his Majesty was still offended at that Assembly holden at St. Andrews. For removing of that offence the Moderator aforesaid would have had the Article of kneeling voted in the conference without reasoning. But after much business and earnest dealing, the said Article by plurality of votes was put to reasoning. For clearing the state of the question, the Ministers defenders of the established order, required again that the said Articles might be extended to the full, and put in perfect form. 2. That the party of the other judgment, would prove them necessary and expedient for our Church, according to the revealed rule, *Affirmanti incumbit probatio*: or otherwise improve our former order already established, as defective, superfluous or confused. 3. That time and place might be granted to all, having calling and interest to reason freely, and hear reasoning in presence of the Assembly for their better direction. 4. That the reasons of moment might be proponed and answered in writing, and some few of either side appointed to put them in due form and order.

The Moderator notwithstanding of the reference of these conditions to the privy conference, rejected them: and as for the party pursuer, and party defender in the reasoning, he determined by himself, that the Minister's defenders of the established order must either prove the Articles to be impious and unlawful, or else they must prove disobedient to his Majesty. It was replied, that poor subjects neither ought, nor conveniently could dispute a question so affected with disobedience to their Sovereign, as was there alleged. But if reformation be intended, and the truth of the Articles proponed be sincerely to be searched so far forth as they may prove good and expedient for this Church; the order agreed upon by his Majesty at Perth 1597 cannot of reason be refused, viz. That matters touching reformation of external government be proponed, *ordine & decenter animo aedificandi, non tentandi*, for searching the truth the undoubted ground of true unity. Notwithstanding of whatsoever could be alleged, the Ministers standing for their possession, were forced to be pursuers, and either to object against the said Articles, or else to be reputed disobedient to his Majesty, and to have no reason on their side. The time being spent, some few reasons were alleged by the Ministers, which were cut off rather by caviling and quarrelling at men's persons, then solidly answered. The conference was appointed in the morning at eight hours, notwithstanding the said hour had been appointed for the second Session of the Assembly.

Wednesday the 26th of August, the second day of the Assembly.

The privy conference convened at 8 hour in the morning. Much time was spent with the Bishops discourses, and other preparations for making way to summary reasoning. Some few Arguments were proponed by the Ministers against kneeling in the act of receiving the sacramental elements of bread and wine; but answered as before. The pretended Moderator to cut off reasoning instantly required, that kneeling might be voted in the conference. The Ministers alleged that the proper use of the conference is to prepare and put in order matters that are to be entreated in the face of the Assembly; and therefore required that the Articles might be formed: and after long debate it was concluded by plurality of votes, that they should be formed. The rest of this short time was spent in naming of Bishops and Doctors for forming and extending the Articles and Acts that were to pass thereupon. The conference was appointed to convene at 4 afternoon.

The Assembly being frustrate of their diet in the morning, assembled at 4 afternoon at the call of the Bell, by the Moderator's expectation. He shewed unto them, that that hour was appointed for the conference allanerly [only]. But seeing they convened, he thought good to make known to them, that the four Articles formerly condescended upon at Aberdeen and St. Andrews, as also the fifth Article against kneeling, after long reasoning were concluded in the conference, and ordained to be formed and produced before them. And so he desired them to depart to the end that matters might be exped [completed], for ending the Assembly [in] the morn. But opposition was made in the contrary, that kneeling was not voted, and the other four Articles were neither reasoned nor voted. After the removal of the Assembly, the act of kneeling as it was formed, was read in presence of the conference. The pretended Moderator urged that kneeling should be voted. It was answered, that it was an intolerable novelty in this Church, a great prejudice to persons, purposes, and privileges, and a presumptuous usurpation of a few to vote and conclude under the colorable pretence of a conference, matters of weight belonging to the whole Church. They required therefore that according to order, reasoning and voting might be reserved to the full Assembly. The pretended Moderator answered, first, that it was the custom of the Lords, of the Articles in parliament to proceed after that manner. Next, that he would not spare to commit twenty prejudices to please the King. And thus kneeling was put in voting without regard of the Assembly, and concluded by plurality of votes. The rest of this short time was spent in talking upon Symony[1], the planting of the Church of Edinburgh, and order to be taken with beggars. The conference appointed the Assembly to convene the morn after Sermon.

Thursday the 27th of August, the third day of the Assembly.

William, B. of Galloway made a Sermon, his Text *Romans 14:19*. His doctrine was far contrary to that which he taught before the estates of Parliament *Anno* 1606. He set at naught the ancient order of our Church, sometime highly commended by himself, and extolled his new light. He presumed to teach them a new kind of Catechism, under whom he himself might be as yet catechized. The second and last Session of this assembly began after dinner and ended this day.

The King's Commissioners, and the Bishops, masters of this Assembly, determined to end all this afternoon: and having the assize [assembly] enclosed for that effect, assured them that out of that house they should not go until his Majesty

---

[1] [The practice of buying or selling ecclesiastical benefices]

were satisfied of his desire. The pretended Moderator earnestly aggreadged [exaggerated] the necessity of yielding and instantly urged present voting without further delay strongly enforcing, that his Majesty behooved to be satisfied, and assuring them, that his Highness would accept of no other answer but yielding. To effectuate his purpose, he blew out many threatnings in most peremptory manner. He insulted upon the ministers assembled, as if they had been hirelings, saying, I know you all well enough. There is never a one of you will suffer so much as the loss of your stipends for the matter. Think not but when the act is made I will get obedience of you. There is none of you that voteth in the contrary mindeth to suffer. Some men, said he, pretend conscience and fear more to offend the people then the King: but all that will not do the turn. Albeit he had formerly affirmed in the case of requiring consent, that although the act were made, his Majesty would be merciful in urging obedience thereto. And they knew him to be more favorable to his brethren then any Bishop of England. He took it also upon his conscience, though it was not true that there was neither lass nor lad, rich nor poor in Scotland some few precise persons excepted, who were not only content but also wished that order of kneeling to be received: whereof he had proof and experience in his own city of St. Andrews, and in this Town since he came hither. He made mention of a pamphlet casten in the pulpit at Edinburgh, wherein it should have been affirmed, that the Bishops were bringing in Papistry, and that good professors will fight in defense of their own religion. By way of answer thereto, he confessed that the ceremonies make not the separation betwixt us and the Roman Church, but their Idolatry, the which if the Romanists would forsake, they would meet them mid-way, and join with them. And as if the Ministers had known any such professors disposed to fight for the religion, or had been of purpose to join with them, he dissuades them to lean to such words, for he had seen the like of that before time at the

17th day of December. He wished if such a thing should happen, it would please his Majesty to make him a Captain, never any of these braggers would come to the field.

After these blasts and terrors, the Ministers with modest importunity insisted that the matters depending might be better cleared by further reasoning and advisement; so much the rather, because these matters had not been reasoned in full Assembly, for the information of all that had interest. After much dealing, and many earnest speeches and desires to be heard, some fashion of liberty was granted to a few, but with such checks and limitations to the party that preased [pressed] to propone and reason, that quickly they were cut off and sorely rebuked, rather borne down with authority, then satisfied with reason. His Majesty's chief Commissioner, & pretended Moderator, straightly enjoined them either to propone a new reason, or else to hold their peace, when as the argument either had not been proponed in conference; or if proponed, not answered; or if answered, not suffered to be replied unto. And suppose all this had been done in the conference, yet all was new to the full Assembly, and ought to have been repeated and fully discussed for information of all voters. Yea many Ministers had not so much as access to hear or propone one argument: they had no seats provided for them, as the other party had: Gentlemen thronged in before them. The defenders of the Articles were permitted to discourse as long as they pleased, to gibe, mock, and cavil, so light account made they of the matters in hand, or the fearful schism ensuing upon such disorders, that their behavior was offensive to the beholders. The best arguments and answers were taken from the authority of the King's sword. He will ranverse [overthrow] all, except we yield; or the authority of his word; as when it was alleged out of Zanchius upon the fourth commandment, that things indifferent abused to Idolatry should be altogether removed. The pretended Moderator opponed [opposed] the judgment of the King of Great Britain, to the judgment of Zanchius, or any of the learned. In a word, the pretended Moderator professed plainly, that neither their reasons nor their number should carry away the matter. These Articles must be concluded, and should be concluded, although there were none but the eleven Bishops, with the authority of his Majesty's Commissioners, they shall impose them. After some few reasons proponed and answered, as is said, it was confessed, that if his Majesty could have been pleased, or put off, they would have reasoned against these Articles, and the introducing of them in this Church. Doctor Lyndesay being posed in conscience, confessed that they had neither reason, nor Scripture, nor Antiquity for them, yet to avert the King's wrath of this Church, yielding was best. Kneeling was chiefly agitate [debated]. Some velitation [discussion] there was made against Holy days. Nothing spoken of the three other Articles, boasting and posting confounded all.

The ministers not being permitted to reason and pursue their arguments verbally with such liberty, as of reason should have been granted, and fearing prejudice in voting, gave in some difficulties in writing, to be considered and removed, before the articles should pass in voting, like as they were ready, if place had been granted to present in writing particular reasons against every one of the said articles, as was plainly professed. But for cutting them short of that intention, the presenter of the said difficulties in a boasting manner was commanded to subscribe the same, and rebuked as not having commission. They suspected a protestation, against the proceedings of this Assembly, for preventing whereof they had declaimed before against the protestation subscribed at the last parliament, as treasonable, and seditious. But when it was perceived, that he sought a penne for subscribing of the same, the Moderator received them. Two of them was read, but no ways respected; the rest were suppressed.

The ministers notwithstanding of the preceding terrors most humbly and earnestly requested his Majesty's

Commissioners, that the concluding of the articles might be continued, which their reasons in writing were sent to his Majesty, and answer returned. But this humble request was despised.

Before the roll was called, his Majesty's letter was read again in open audience of the said assembly, no doubt to the end the last impression might incline the voters to consent. The minister's defenders of the established order required again, that none might have place to vote, but such as were authorized with lawful commission: but that order could not be admitted. Yea the pretended Moderator answered, that if al Scotland were there present they should have vote.

The question put in voting was thus formed. Whether will ye consent to these articles, or disobey the King? The words chosen to distinguish the votes were: *agree: disagree: non liquet.* The question proponed was affected with this strait condition: he that denieth one, denieth all. The question being thus contrived, the Moderator certified them, that whosoever voted against the articles, his name should be marked and given up to his Majesty. For gathering the votes, he took the roll in his own hand from the Clarke, to whom of office it belongs so to mark the votes, that accordingly he may form the acts truly as his oath and office bindeth him. First were called his highness' commissioners, and their assessors; then the Noblemen, Bishops, and Barons; then the Doctors and Ministers, last of all the burgesses. The Doctors and Ministers were called on without order. He called first on those, of whom he was assured to be on the affirmative side without respect of the order of Province or Presbytery, as for example, the Arch Deacon of St. Andrews and M^r. Patrik Galloway a man of many pensions were ranked with the Ministers of the North. Some wanting commission were called and voted affirmative: diverse others having commission of whose negative they were assured; were omitted. In calling on the names, he inculcate[d] these and the like words: have the King in your mind: remember of the King: look to the King. In the end by plurality of votes the five articles were concluded and consented unto. 1. Kneeling in the act of receiving the sacramental elements of bread and wine. 2. Five holy days: the day of Christ's nativity, Passion, Resurrection, Ascension, and the Pentecost. 3. Episcopal confirmation. 4. Private Baptism. 5. Private communion. His Majesty's Commissioners and their assessors: all the noble men, except one: all the Barons except one: all the Doctors except D. Strang: all the Burgesses and a number of Ministers voted affirmative; one noble man, one Doctor, and forty-five Ministers voted negative: some few, *non liquet.*

THE NULLITY OF PERTH ASSEMBLY

The general Assembly hath usually met, since the reformation of the religion, according to the indiction of time and place made by the former Assembly. And if it happened that any Assembly was to be holden *Pro re nata*, premonition was made in dew time by his Majesty, and the Commissioners of the Church, and the occasions set down expressly, to the effect Commissioners might be sent instructed according to the quality of the business to be entreated. Nevertheless after diverse reports given out by such as stand in credit in Church affaires, that his Majesty was so incensed against the last Assembly holden at St. Andrews that there was no hope of any other Assembly: This Assembly beyond expectation was proclaimed to be holden within twenty days after the proclamation made at the market cross of Edinburgh, without any advertisement given to the Presbyteries anent the matters to be handled.

The act of chattouris of old were void, and of none effect, when the meanest member having vote was neglected, contemned, or not lawfully warned. Such like the act of Provincial synods, when the meanest suffragan [bishop] was not regarded with lawful citation, according to the rule *Contemptus unius plus obest, quam multorum contradictio*. Nevertheless for lack of lawful warning and convenient space to provide and prepare Commissioners, there was absent from that Assembly, four dioceses viz. Orknay, Caithness, Argyle, and the Isles, beside diverse presbyteries, whose interest was as proper and necessary in the general assembly as of any suffragan [bishop] or particular member in the chapter.

The general assembly, the highest judicatory Ecclesiastical within this realm, hath ever after exhortation made by the last Moderator lyted [nominated], and lawfully elected a new Moderator according to diverse acts continual custom and practice of this Church. The which presbyteries hath been so regarded, that the convention holden at Perth by his Majesty's missive the last of February, 1596 although frequented by his Majesty's presence with a great number of the nobility, Barons and Burgesses with the Commissioners from every presbytery was for the defect aforesaid no further acknowledged to be a lawful Assembly, then the general Assembly holden at Dundee the year following 1597 declared the same, that is, to be a lawful extraordinary Assembly. Nevertheless no moderator was lawfully elected in this Assembly, but the place usurped by him who had practiced against the matter there proposed, and not as yet determined, and consequently, who ought to have been secluded from any authority in respect of the prejudice committed by him.

By order established, acts standing in force and continual custom free of all controversy and quarrel, all and every one of the ordinary members of a general Assembly, having place and power to vote, or capable of moderation, are and should be authorized with lawful commissions from inferior Assemblies viz. Presbyteries, Burghs and Universities, according to the act made *Anno* 1537. Nevertheless the Bishops, a great number of noble men and Barons, and some Ministers, having no lawful commission presumed to carry themselves as lawful members of the said Assembly.

Whereas the proceedings of the Assembly ought to be free without preoccupation either with terrors or allurements. This Assembly was preoccupied with Sermons, Letters, harangues, with allurements on the one side, and terrors on the other.

No other ought to be chosen members of the privy conference but such as are authorized with commission to be members of the Assembly. Nevertheless the pretended moderator did nominate for the privy conference such as he pleased, before the commissions were delivered, and consequently not duly informed, who were the just members of the Assembly.

According to the rule, *Totum est maius sua parte*, the Assembly is greater then the conference: and according to another rule *Turpis pars omnis toti non congrua*. It is an absurd conference that disagrees from the whole Assembly, Nevertheless in that Assembly some few named by the pretended Moderator, not chosen by the Assembly, not only according to the custom of the privy conference concurred with the said Moderator for preparing and digesting of matters to be proponed in dew order, but took upon them to reason, vote, and conclude the matters properly belonging to the whole Assembly.

It had been the commendable care of Godly Emperors, and their honorable deput[ie]s in general Councils, to provide that nothing be done violently, nor extorted by terror, but that time and liberty be granted for reasoning upon matters proponed and that the book of God be laid open for finding out the truth. Agatho writing to the Emperor Constantine adviseth him to grant free power of speaking to every one that desires to speak for his faith which he believeth, and holdeth that all men may evidently see that no man willing or desirous to speak for the truth was forbidden, hindered or rejected by any force, threatnings, terror, or whatsoever else might avert them from so doing. Conform to this advice, the Emperor answereth as followeth. By God almighty we favor no party, but shall keep ourselves equal to all, no way making necessity in any point. Nevertheless in this assembly, the necessity of yielding was enforced under no less pains then the wrath of authority, imprisonment, exile, deprivation of Ministers, and utter subversion of the estate and order of this Church. Such as by the providence of God had their mouths opened to reason, were checked, quarreled, rebuked, boasted, interrupted, and for their discouragement, it was plainly professed that neither the reasoning nor the number of voters should carry the matter away. The party defender was forced to pursue. The collecting and putting in order of the reasons of either side was refused.

In free and lawful assemblies private reasoning is not sufficient, but it is requisite that there be also free reasoning in public for the full information of all who have the right of voting. Nevertheless in this assembly public reasoning was hardly obtained, and when it was obtained, it was not full and free to propone, and pursue with replies.

In all free and lawful assemblies, humble requests for mature deliberation in maters of great importance hath been heard, & granted. But in this assembly humble supplication for continuation till matters were more ripely considered, or till his Majesty's answer was returned to the petition of the defenders of the established order, was peremptorily refused.

Pope Leo excepteth against the second Council of Ephesus, call Praedatory, that Dioscorus, who challenged the chief place, keepeth not Priestly moderation and would not suffer the synodal letters of the West to be read. In all free and lawful Assemblies good advisements hath been heard & followed. But in this Assembly some difficulties presented in writing to be considered and removed before the voting, were peremptorily rejected.

In all free and lawful Assemblies public voting should be free of all terrors according to the rule, *nihil consensui tam contrarium est, quam vis atque metus quem comprobare contra bonos mores est*. Nevertheless in this Assembly, his Majesty's letters were read the fourth time, immediately before the public voting, to move the Assembly. The pretended Moderator threatened to mark their names who dissented, and breathed out many terrors and threatnings, and so he made good in public, that which he professed in private, that he would commit twenty prejudices to further his Majesty's purpose.

In all free and lawful Assemblies the estate of the question to be voted, ought to be so formed that it carry with it no danger. Nevertheless in this Assembly the matter to be voted was proponed with sensible danger, agree, or be reputed disobedient to his Majesty, that is, either make a constitution to bind all Ministers, and professors of this reformed Kirk to return to these five articles which they have vomited, or else ye shall be reputed disobedient.

As the acts which are to pass in voting should be distinguished in number: clear in order, particularly expressed from point to point, because they should contain directions of certain actions to be performed, &c. So the matters offered to voting should be distinctly, clearly, and particularly proponed. Nevertheless in this Assembly all was shut up in a confused caption *a multis interrogatis*, and voted at once voting in one session. Justly therefore may their conclusions be called *Leges Satura*.

In all free Assemblies such order is observed in calling the names of the voters, that no public prejudice be committed. Nevertheless in this Assembly neither the accustomed order of Provinces, nor Presbyteries was observed; but such were called on first, as were known to be affirmative voters, to discourage and disperse the negatives.

Leo saith Epist. 25 that some that came to the Council of Ephesus were rejected, and others were brought in who at the pleasure of Dioscorus were brought to yield captive hands to their impious subscriptions. For they knew it would be prejudicial to their estate, unless they did such things as were enjoined them. It is *crimine falsi* in gathering of votes, either to pass by them, who have place and power to vote, or to admit such as are not lawfully authorized. Nevertheless in this Assembly not only were some past by who were known resolved to vote negative, but diverse others also disposed to vote affirmative were admitted, or rather brought in without commission.

In all free and lawful Assemblies, not only Ministers, but all others of whatsoever rank, ought to be authorized, with commission, or else they have not the power of voting.

Nevertheless in this Assembly, persons of all ranks not authorized with commission, were admitted to vote, as may be seen by the induction following.

It hath pleased his Majesty in former times to send but some few Commissioners in his Highness' absence, to concur with the Assembly, and to propone his Highness desire thereunto, &c. Nevertheless in this Assembly, not only his Majesty's Commissioners, but also their Assessors gave every one vote, whereas his Majesty's self being present; never claimed further, then the power of one vote.

At Edinburgh in July 1568 it was ordained that Barons should be chosen Commissioners in Synodal assemblies. At Dundee in March 1597 after the full establishment of Presbyteries, it was appointed in presence of his Majesty, that Barons should be chosen Commissioners with consent of Presbyteries, and that one Baron only should be directed out of the bounds of a Presbytery. Nevertheless in this Assembly, the Noblemen and Barons had neither commission according to the old act, nor according to the new.

In the year of God 1568 it was ordained that Burgesses should be chosen Commissioners by the Council and Kirk-session of their Burgh conjunctly, and in the year 1597 that they should be chosen with consent of the Presbytery. Item, that every Burgh have power to direct but one Commissioner, except Edinburgh, to whom it was permitted to direct two. Nevertheless in this Assembly, neither of the said acts were observed.

At Montrose 1600 it was statuted and ordained, that none of them who shall have vote in Parliament in the name of the Church, shall come as Commissioners to the general Assembly, nor have any vote in the same unless they be authorized with commission from their own Presbyteries to that effect. This act was never repealed, no not at the pretended assembly holden at Glasgow, but by the said assembly they stand countable to every general assembly for their proceedings. Howbeit the Presbyteries were spoiled of their authority in many things at the said pretended assembly: yet of the power of election of Commissioners they were not spoiled. Neither is there any other order of election of Commissioners, and constitution of the members of the assembly set down by any act of our Kirk, then was established *Anno* 1597. Nevertheless in this assembly, they not only presented themselves without commission, but sat as Lords over-ruling it. They had practiced the ceremonies against the established laws before they were proponed to the Assembly, they ought therefore to have been secluded and sharply censured; but they usurped the place both of Judge and party.

At St. Andrews in April 1582 it was thought expedient that Presbyteries should not be astricted [bound] to direct their Moderator in commission, but whom they judged fittest for the purpose. That constant Moderators should be constant members of the general assembly, is a forged clause foisted in an act of a pretended assembly holden at Linlithquow the year of God 1606 the which assembly neither the Church then did, nor the Bishops now will stand to. Nevertheless in this assembly, some Moderators of Presbyteries voted without election, and only by virtue of the forged clause of the act aforesaid. If any Presbytery directed their Moderators in commission upon ignorance and error, having respect to the forged clause aforesaid. Their ignorance and error is not lawful consent. It is in the mean time to be remembered, that the present Moderators are not of the quality of these constant Moderators, but of a new Edition set out at Glasgow, viz. They are the Bishop's Deputes placed by them in Presbyteries.

The Assessors to his Majesty's Commissioners, the Noblemen, Barons, Bishops, Burgesses, and Moderators imposed upon Presbyteries with some Ministers voting without warrant, being subtracted from the number of affirmative voters, the negatives will not be found inferior in number to the affirmatives authorized with commission. And suppose inferior in number, yet not in weight, for the negative voters adhered to the judgment of the Church, heard no reasons for the novelties proposed, were not overcome with persuasions or terrors, as was the affirmatives.

The affirmative voters authorized with commission, either had their commissions procured by their Bishops, or else were mercenary Pensioners or Plat-servers for augmentation of stipends: or gapers for promotion: or of suspect credit for benefits received or hoped for, or had subscribed other private Articles in private more dangerous then the present Articles: or had been threatened privately by their own diocesian Bishops with deposition: or were not well informed in their judgment for lack of full and free reasoning: or were circumvented with promises made to them, by their Bishops, that they should not be urged with the practice, if they would only consent to make an act to please the King: or were terrified with the public threatnings before mentioned. Judge therefore whether their votes should be pondered or numbered.

In omnil us causis pro facto accipitur id in quo quis alium terrefacit quo minus fiat. In this Assembly the affirmative voters confessed that they assented not simpliciter [unrestricted] to the Articles proposed as knowing truths, but only to avert the wrath of authority, standing in their own Judgment against them, and not for them, in respect of the estate of this church. Hence it may be clearly seen that their votes were only affirmative in respect of their fear, but negative in respect of their judgment, and dutiful affection to this Church.

Other informalities may be observed, but these are sufficient to prove the nullity of this pretended Assembly whereby the established estate of this Church is so far prejudged, or rather simple people for their facility endangered, if they upon the pretended authority of this Assembly shall adventure to make defection from their former profession confirmed by so many and well advised Assemblies, and blessed by the experience of God's great love in his best benefits, or to violate their solemn oath, and subscription. The pretender may as safely profess that he will alter his profession, or violate his oath, and subscription, suppose there had been no Assembly at all. But to detain simple people in their bygone revolt, it will be cried out and inculcat[ed] that some few persons (and to make them odious they will be called mall-contents, troublers of the estate, seditious persons, and what not? for the which contumelies and reproaches account must be made one day) that they may not, nor should not judge upon the nullity of the Assemblies. It is true by way of jurisdiction or superordination (as they call it) no private man should presume so to do, for that judgment belongeth to another free, and lawful Assembly. But by the judgment of discretion every Christian man ought to judge how matters of religion are imposed upon him, and by what authority. If thou mayest not discern as a judge, thou mayest discern as a Christian. If ye shall admit indifferently whatsoever is concluded under the glorious name of an Assembly, then may we be brought to admit not only the English ceremonies, but also Lutheranism, and Papistry. If Ministers give way to their Parishioners to practice the obtruded Ceremonies at their pleasures, if sworn professors entangle themselves again with the superfluities, whereof the Lord hath made them free, let the one and the other take heed how they defend themselves from the just challenge of back sliding, and the rest of the inconveniences, that may ensue on their change.

If the Parliament by acts, authorize matters affected with such informalities, and nullities, matters of themselves so contrary to our profession, their ratification of a vicious thing cannot be a rule to a Christian man's conscience. But it is to be hoped, that the Lord shall so dispose the hearts of stats-men to the love of the truth, quietness of the Church and Country, and peace of men's consciences, that no unreasonable burthen shall be knit upon the members of Christ's body by any deed of theirs under the name of a benefit to the Church. *Invito beneficium non datur.*

Consider three things: first the nullity of this Assembly. 2. Thy own oath and subscription, how it admits or abhors this change suppose the Assembly had been lawful. 3. If the particulars offered can be made lawful, or expedient by any Assembly whatsoever.

THE ARTICLES PRESENTED TO
the Assembly August 27th with some quotations added for confirmation.

For so much as we have been debarred of access, and from hearing the proceedings of the conference, their reasonings, consultations, and advisements, anent the Articles proposed to this general Assembly: whereof all and every one of them so nearly toucheth us in our Christian resolution and offices of our Ministry. In most humble manner we present to your considerations the particulars here after specified, in the fear of God entreating your favorable answer to the same.

1. The articles proposed, if they be concluded, they do innovate and bring under the slander of change the estate of this Church, so advisedly established by Ecclesiastical constitutions, acts of parliament, approbation of other Kirks, and good liking of the best reformed Christians without and within this kingdom, and so evidently blessed with happy success and sensible experience of God's greatest benefits by the space of 58 years, and above; so that we may boldly say to the praise of God that no Church hath enjoyed the truth and purity of religion in larger liberty. And upon some such considerations, it pleased his gracious Majesty to continue the Church of England in her established estate, as may be seen in the conference at Hampton Court, and Thomas Sparke his book written there upon. *Ipsa quippe mutatio, etiam quae adiuvat utilitate novitate perturbat: quapropter quae utilis non est, perturbatione infructuosa consequenter noxia est,* saith Augustine Epist. 118. That is even a change that is helpful for utility, perturbeth with the novelty. Wherefore consequently a change that is not profitable, is noisome through fruitless perturbation. Rather a Kirk with some fault, then still a change, it is said in the conference at Hampton court.

2. The receiving again of these articles so justly rejected, and so carefully, and long kept forth of this Kirk, grieveth reformed professors tenderly affected to our reformation, and giveth occasion to our adversaries to reprove our separation from them, of rashness, levity, and inconstancy, and not only hindereth their conversion, but strengthens their hope of our further conformity with them. *Quoties non mutarunt suam quisque senteniam? Quod aedificant body, cras destruunt. Hodie lapidem locant in fundamentum, coementoque confirmant, quem postero dic eruunt, & conterunt. Vbique revocationes, emendationes, novi foetus, aliae atque aliae, quoties nova sententia placet, assertiones: alius deturbat alium, confusio confusioni permiseetur: atque interim scinditur incertu studis in contraria vulgus. Nec adhuc cernimus aliud, est quis nisi mente captus dicat istiusmodi artifices reaedificare Ecclesia Dei, quibus omnia incerta fluxa, instablia, contraria: quibus nulla dogmatum constantia, nulla animorum consensio,* Antdidagma Coloniens, Page 4. That is, How oft have they not changed every one their opinion: that which they build today, they demolish tomorrow: they place this day a stone for a foundation, and make it sure with mortar which they pull up the day following and bruise in pieces: every where there is revocations, corrections, new births, diverse assertions, as oft as a new opinion pleaseth any of them: One throweth down another: Confusion is mingled with confusion; and in the mean time, the doubtful vulgars are severed in contrary factions. Neither do we as yet perceive any other thing: and who will say except such a one as is beside himself, that such artisans reedifies the Kirk of God, to whom all things are uncertain, flowing, unstable, contrary, who have no constancy in the heads of doctrine no consent of minds. &c.

3. They cannot stand in one profession with brotherly kindness, peace, and love which must be tenderly kept amongst the members of Christ's body, as the same consists of stronger, and more infirm as may appear in the apostolic rules following. First, *all things are lawful to me, but all things are not*

profitable. I may do all things but I will not be brought under the power of any thing. 2. Let every man be fully persuaded in his own mind. 3 Whatsoever is not of faith is sin. 4 Let every one understand according to sobriety as God hath dealt to every man the measure of faith. 5 Take heed least by any means this power of yours be an occasion of falling to them that are weak. 6 Through thy knowledge shall thy weak brother fall, for whom Christ died. 7 When ye sin against the brethren, and wound their weak consciences, ye sin against Christ. 8 Whatsoever ye do, do all to the glory of God. 9. Give no offence, neither to the Jew nor to the Grecian, nor to the Kirk of God. 10 Please all men in all things, not seeking your own profit, but the profit of many that they may be saved. 11 Cause not your commodity to be evil spoken of. 12. Let all things be done, honestly, and in order. Things indifferent (put the case man's invention were of that nature) in the case of scandal, cease to be indifferent, and are as things moral. Perkins, *Galatians 2:3*.

4. They give way to human inventions, and bring the wrong key of mans wit within the house of God whereby toys and trifling Ceremonies in number and force are multiplied as men's wits are variable to invent. Who requires those things at your hands.

5. The admitting of some openeth the door to the rest, and the multitude of such make us inferior to the Jews in two respects. 1. Their Ceremonies were all divine. 2. In number fewer then ritual Christians do observe betwixt the Pasche [Passover], and the Pentecost, Gerson complaineth, *quod multitudine levissimarum ceremoniarum vis omnis Spiritus Sancti quem in nobis vigere oportuit, & vera Pietas, Sit extincta*. That with the multitude of frivolous ceremonies true piety was extinguished and the force of the Spirit which ought to be powerful in us. *Jewel Apollog. Pag. 116. Sed quamvis hoc neque inveniri possit, quomodo contra fidem sunt, ipsam tamen religionem servilibus oneribus premunt, ut tolerabillior sit conditio Iudœorum, qui etiamsi tempus libertatis non agnoverint, legalibus tamen sarcinis, non humanis presumtionibus subjiciuntur. August. Epist. 119.* Howbeit it cannot be found how they are contrary to the faith, yet they press down religion itself with servile burdens,

so that the estate of the Jews is more tolerable, who howbeit they did now acknowledge the time of their liberty, are subject notwithstanding to the burdens of the Law, not to the presumptions of man.

Quanto majus accedit cumulo rituum in Ecclesia, tanto majus detrahitur, non tantum lil ertati Christianae, sed & Christo, et ejus fidei. Confes. Orthodox. Cap 27. That is, The more that the heap of rites and Ceremonies in the Kirk increaseth, the more is derogated, not only from Christian liberty, but also from Christ and his faith. Learned and grave men may like better of the single form of policy in our Kirk, then of the many ceremonies of the Kirk of England. Epistle before Basilicon Doron.

6. Matters of that nature bring inevitably with them disputations, divisions, contentions as may be seen in all Kirks, where such coals of contention gets entry. The Pasche of the Primitive Kirk, The Interim of Germany, the rent of the Kirk of England, our own experience since the strife of the external gubernation [governing] began among us &c.

7. They hinder edification, for how meckle [much] time and zeal shall be spent upon the inbringing and establishing of these, as much leisure and opportunity shall Satan get to sow and water the tares of Atheism, Schism, Popery, and dissention. Consider the sentences following. 1. *Let us proceed by one rule, that we may mind one thing. Philippians 3:16. 2. Let us follow the truth in love, and in all things grow up in him, who is the head, that is Christ. Ephesians 4:3. Give no place to the Devil. 4. If ye be otherwise minded God shall reveal the same to you. 5. Feed my sheep. 6. Take heed to your selves and to the flock. 7. Let no root of bitterness spring up to trouble you. 8. Fulfill my joy that ye be like minded, having the same love being of one accord and of one judgment, that nothing be done through contention or vain glory, but that in meekness of mind every man esteem other better then himself. 9. Do all things without murmuring and reasoning. 10. It was needful for me to write unto you, that ye should earnestly contend for the faith, which was once given to the Saints. 11. While*

men slept the enemy came, sowed his tares amongst the wheat, and went his way.

8. They bring a sensible blot either upon the happy memory of our godly and wise predecessors, in so far as we depart from that reformation, so wisely brought in, appointed & established by them, or else upon ourselves, by resuming again of dangerous superfluities without reason, rejected by them, for weighty and necessary causes, *Magnum est hoc Dei munus, quod una est religionem puram, et eutaxian, doctrinae videlicet retinendae vinculum, in Scotiam intulistis. Sic obsecro et obtestor, haec duo simul retinete, ut uno amisso alterum non diu permanere posse semper memineritis.* Beza epistle to M. Knox. This is a great benefit of God that ye have brought into Scotland true religion and good order, the band that retaineth doctrine, at one time, so I beseech you and obtest [entreat] that ye retain these two together, so that ye remember, that if the one be lost, the other cannot endure long. And again he saith *quam recte illud, quod disciplinam simul cum doctrina conjungitis, obsecro, et obtestor ut ita pergatis ne vobis idem quod tam multis eveniat, ut qui in limine impegerint progredi non possunt, immo etiam interdum ne velint quidem, quod longè miserimum est*. How well was that done, that ye conjoined Doctrine and Discipline together, I beseech you and obtest [entreat], that ye go forward, lest it happen to you which is befallen to many, that could not make a progress, having stumbled in the very entry, yea sometime were not willing which is most lamentable.

9. They set loose the filthy minds and mouths of fleshly livers to triumph against the most sound and best reformed professors, and to rejoice in their rotten opinions, and restored opportunities of sensual observations of guising, gluttony, carrels, &c.

10. They are declared by this Church to be contrary doctrine, as may be seen in the 1st, 2nd and 3rd chapters of the first book of Discipline, in these words: We judge that all doctrine repugnant to the Evangel, should be utterly

suppressed as damnable to man's salvation. In the books of Old and New Testament we affirm that all things necessary for the instruction of the Kirk, and to make the man of God perfect, is contained and sufficiently expressed. By contrary doctrine we understand, whatsoever men by Laws, Councils, or Constitutions have imposed on the consciences of men without the express commandment of God's word, as keeping of holy days commanded by man, the feast of Christmas, and other feasts.

11. The Commissioners of Presbyteries here convened sufficiently understand, that neither the Presbyteries from whom they have their commissions, nor the particular Churches of this Realm either require, are willing, or consent to admit these notations. *Consitentur Theologi nihil esse per Synodos Ecclesijs invitis obtrudendum.* The Divines do confess that nothing should be obtruded upon Churches against their will.

12. The Commissioners of Presbyteries here assembled, understanding the alienation of them from whom they received commission, from these Articles, can by no warrant oblige nor bind their unwilling Presbyteries, and Congregations to their votes. *Ecclesiam dissentienlem & invitam obligare quis potest?* Who can bind a Church disassenting and unwilling.

13. There stand in force divers acts of parliament in favor of our present order, Ia. 6. Parl. 1. cap. 8, Ia. 6. Parl. 6. cap. 68. & cap. 69. Item, the first act of the Parliament *Anno* 1592.

14. The Ministers of this Church by order of the same printed and inserted before the Psalm book at their admissions respective promise in the presence of God, and of his congregation assembled, to abhor and utterly to refuse all doctrine alleged necessary unto salvation, that is not expressly contained in the Old and New Testament, and according to the graces and utterances that God shall grant unto them to profess, instruct, and maintain the purity of the doctrine contained in the sacred word of God, and to the uttermost of

their power to gainstand [withstand], and convince the gainsayers, and teachers of men's inventions. Item, to submit themselves most willingly to the wholesome Discipline of this Kirk, by the which they were then called to the office and charge, promising in God's presence obedience to all admonitions, secretly or publicly given, &c.

15. The subscribers of the confession of faith by their oath therein contained, promise and swear to continue in the obedience of the doctrine and discipline of this Church, and to defend the same according to their vocation and power, all the days of their lives, under the pains contained in the Law, and danger both of body and soul in the day of God's fearful judgment: and to abhor and detest all contrary religions, but chiefly all kind of Papistry in general, even as they are now damned and confuted by the word of God and Kirk of Scotland, but in special the Popes five bastard Sacraments, whereof Confirmation is one, with all rites, ceremonies, and false doctrines added to the true Sacraments without the word of God: his absolute necessity of Baptism, &c. Which confession and practice following thereupon, is come to the eyes of the world in print, and solemnly renewed in the covenant celebrated in the general and provincial Assemblies, Presbyteries, and Kirk-sessions in the year of God 1596. And how shall any man be heard to speak against that whereunto he hath formerly sworn and subscribed? See the conference at Hampton-court. For the better understanding of their last Articles, I will set down a short discussion of the Oath.

THE OATH DISCUSSED

The Religion, Doctrine, and Discipline received, believed, and defended by the Kirk of Scotland, and namely the public ministration of Baptism, and the Lord's Supper, sitting at the table in the act of the receiving the bread and wine of that Sacrament, the observation of the Lord's Day, and the examination of children, for the first time at the ninth year of their age, for the second at the twelfth, for the third at the fourteenth, excluding and abhorring private baptism, private communion, kneeling in the act of receiving the Supper, holy days, or feasts of Christmas, Passion, Resurrection, Ascension, and sending down of the Holy Ghost: were brought in at the reformation of religion, and enjoyed ever since in manner and form as follows.

After due trial and advisement taken of the heads in general and particular above written, the whole Church was of one heart and judgment concerning the same, and every man was permitted to hear reasoning, and such as would were permitted to reason, every man professed himself to be persuaded in his own mind.

The particulars to be embraced and followed, and the corruptions to be avoided, were by Ecclesiastical authority in free, full, and lawful general Assemblies, public confessions, and solemn protestations advisedly established.

The estates of Parliament agreeing in judgment with the Kirk concerning the said matters by their acts ratified and approved the Kirk constitutions, and appointed civil penalties against the transgressors of the same, with provision of order whereby they might be called, convicted, and punished.

The said unity of judgment authorized by the constitutions of the Kirk, and laws of the Country, and the whole particulars established by these bands, having been tried by practice, and other ways, have proved expedient, profitable and necessary by the space of fifty-nine years, and now justly have acquired the force of good and commendable custom.

For our further confirmation of the said religion, doctrine, and discipline in general, and in the particulars before named, all and every one of all estates of this Realm have solemnly sworn, that they shall continue in the obedience of the doctrine and discipline of this Church, and shall defend the same according to their vocation and power.

Notwithstanding of these five obligations, viz. unity of judgment, and opinion: Ecclesiastical authority reiterated & confirmed by many famous Assemblies: Many civil laws: Nine and fifty years practice and custom universally commended: and the said solemn oath divers times repeated, the pretended assembly holden last at Perth, received certain forms formerly excluded and abhorred.

Queritur, if one or more Preachers or Professors in the said Kirk, standing to the Kirks former judgment; and able to defend the same by good reason, at least seeing no warrant in the contrary, may dispense with the said oath, or follow the plurality of preachers, & professors dispensing with the same in the assembly. And what power may compel the alteration of judgment, or loose the said oath in any case aforesaid? Leaving the full answer to the wise and well reformed Christian walking before God, and looking for a crown upon the glorious day of our Lord. For present reformation we shall consider the said oath: first in the persons, takers of the same. 2. The matter whereto they swear. 3. The form and manner, whereby they are bound. 4. The force and effect of that form for making sure men's particular deeds.

The persons takers of the oath are all baptized Christians of perfect age, able to examine themselves, and so to eat of the Lord's Supper, honored with callings, and all professors of

Christian fellowship, of Christ the searcher of hearts, and of life and judgment eternal, free of madness, and of all restraint of superior power in this case, understanding perjury and the pains thereof, at their own liberty, and free of all coaction [coercion]: as at length may be seen in the confessions of faith registered in the Acts of Parliament, printed in the book of Discipline before the Psalms in meter, the confession of faith subscribed by the King's Majesty and his household, published by open proclamation and yet standing in print. And in the covenant celebrated by the general and provincial Assemblies, and by the Presbyteries, and particular congregations, but more summarily in the heads underwritten, acknowledged and confessed by themselves.

We all, and every one of us after long and due examination of our consciences in matters of true and false religion are now thoroughly resolved in the truth by the word and Spirit of God.

We believe with our hearts, confess with our mouths, subscribe with our hands, and constantly affirm before God, and the world, that the faith and religion, received, believed, and defended by the Kirk of Scotland, the King's Majesty and three Estates of this realm particularly expressed in the confession of our faith, established and publicly confirmed by sundry acts of parliament, and now of long time hath been openly professed by the King's Majesty, and whole body of this Realm, is only the true Christian faith and religion pleasing God, and bringing salvation to man.

To this confession, and form of religion we willingly agree in our consciences in all points, as unto God's undoubted truth and verity.

We willing to take away all suspicion of hypocrisy and double dealing with God and his Kirk, protest, and call the searcher of hearts for witness, that our minds and hearts do fully agree with this our confession, oath, and subscription.

We protest that we are not moved with any worldly respect, but are persuaded only in our conscience through the knowledge and love of God's true religion printed in our hearts by the Holy Spirit, as we shall answer to him in the day, when the secrets of all hearts shall be disclosed &c.

Before and at the time of their solemn protestations, it was well known to all the promisers, Swearers, Subscribers, that 1. At Edinburgh, the 18th day of October 1581, and from the reformation to that year it was resoled, and by common consent concluded that in time coming no sacrament be administered in private houses, but solemnly according to the good order hitherto observed. 2. At Edinburgh in January 1560, it was declared by this Kirk that Christ sat with his disciples at a table, when he instituted the supper, and that sitting at table was the most convenient gesture to this holy action. 3. That the Pope's five bastard sacraments, whereof Confirmation is one, with all rites ceremonies and false doctrines added to the ministration of the sacraments were abhorred. And that examination of children, after the manner agreed upon in the Kirk, was sufficient to unite baptized infants with the Kirk in the participation of the Lord's Supper. 4. That at Edinburgh in January 1560, the Kirk judged utterly to be abolished from this Realm, keeping of holy days such as the feast of Christmas &c. Imposed upon the consciences of men without warrant of God's word, and many other things of the like nature condemned by preaching, and corrected by public censures of the Kirk. Hence it is evident that no exception can be taken against the persons promising, swearing and subscribing, for dispensing with the said oath.

The matter whereunto they bind themselves by oath is the religion, doctrine and discipline received, believed and defended by the Kirk of Scotland. In respect of this matter, the oath is partly assertory, and partly promissory. They affirm as follows. 1. That it is God's undoubted truth and verity grounded only upon his written word. 2. That it pleaseth God, and bringeth salvation to man. 3. That they are now thoroughly resoled in this truth. 4. That they detest all vain allegories, rites, signs and traditions brought into the Kirk without, or against the word of God and Doctrine of this true reformed Kirk. Such assertions cannot be loosed, an assertory oath cannot be dispensed with, for it is already past. *Assertorij juramenti materia in necessitatem transijt.* They have all already sworn that they are persuaded in their consciences in the points aforesaid. This persuasion is not to be performed, but is already past and sworn. We cannot therefore go in the contrary except we will be perjured. The promissory part is, to continue in the obedience of the doctrine and Discipline of this Kirk, or to defend the same. The endurance of the said continuance and defense is all the days of our lives. The execration whereby they enforce the truth and promise of their oath is, under the pains contained in the law, and danger both of body and soul in the day of God's fearful judgment. This continuance and defense in respect of the worthiness of the matter affirmed, and of the nature of an oath and promise, and in respect of the endurance, and execration adjoined, leaveth no place to allege the events of posterior accidents incident to the matter sworn to, to loose or dispense with the said oath, or promise, as it may be clearly seen in the nature of an oath.

The forms whereby the foresaid persons are bound to continue, and defend the said religion are 1. Public profession before God and the world. 2. Printed and published confessions. 3. Subscription. 4. Obedience to the laws of the Country. 5. Christian subjection to the order of the Kirk. 6. The solemn covenant. Lastly, the oath. All these forms amongst all people, but especially amongst Christians are reputed for strong bands. If we consider the zeal of our Christians to God and his truth, the oath may be called *juramentum affectionis*, the oath of affection. If their willingness to cleave to their brethren in sincerity of profession it is *voluntarium et quasi conventionale*, it is voluntary, and as it were by pact. If their loyalty to his majesty and reverent obedience to the Kirk it is judicial, an oath before a Judge. If suspicion or any other sort of undutifulness, it is *Purgativum*, an oath of purgation. If the fullness of the form, it is not simple, but compound, having a most fearful execration expressed. If ye consider the matter sworn to, viz. The religion, Doctrine, and discipline, as it is affirmed for undoubted truth, it is *assertorium*, an assertory oath. If the continuance in defense of the doctrine and discipline, it is promissory, whereby the particular acts of their future continuance and defense are bound to be established in religion, doctrine, and discipline. In respect of the which establishment and future continuance and defense, it is a thing bygone, and past in *rem judicatam*, worthy of the said continuance and defense, but no ways subject to the changes accessory to the persons by oath indebted to these duties. The matter affirmed in this oath, concerneth God, our brethren and the rest of our own souls in the course of profession. The duty that we perform to God, is to take him to be Judge and witness of our sincerity and constancy of our profession. The duty that we do to our neighbors is to put them in assurance of our brotherly disposition and carriage in the communion of Saints. The honor and the ease that we bring to ourselves is, that we lay, as it were, God in pawn for us who hath the clear knowledge of most secret things, and is the undoubted patron of verity, full of all justice, and power to punish perjury.

The force and effect of this form being considered in the persons swearers upon whom God principally hath laid the law of swearing, should be a strong cord to restrain us from the variable inconstancy and customable changes that falleth in the world for the reasons following. 1. An oath is the golden cord, whereby we are bound to sacred verity, and the sacrificing knife whereby we cut away superfluous controversies. 2. The effect of an oath is a most solemn and sure obligation, and therefore by the consent of all the Doctors the oaths of compulsion, and hurtful, in matters prestable [capable], and not impious, are to be kept. 3. A lawful oath by God alone may be loosed, who is the chief *CUI* [to whom (and)] for whose sake it is taken. 4. It is a note of the Antichrist to dispense with oaths. It was well said, that dispensations *nihil aliud sunt quam legum vulnera*. What is more religious in religion then an oath? What shall be the force of bands or contracts? With what cords shall societies be knit if men shall be freed from their lawful oaths, or rather forced to violate them?

To elude the oath the temporizer objecteth that all oaths of inferiors are made, *salvo jure superiorum*, seeing therefore the King & the Kirk, our superiors, have made those innovations, we are freed of our oath, so far as innovation is made. *Answer.* That an oath made by the inferior, with knowledge and consent of the Superior cannot afterward be loosed by the Superior. The Canonist giveth this example, a scholar is sworn to his Creditor not to depart from the school beyond the bounds and limits agreed on betwixt him and the creditor, before he make payment at the appointed day, his father commands him to return home. If he contracted the debt for his study, he had the tacit consent of his father. For setting him to school, he did assent to all necessaries serving for his studies. The father here is by his own tacit consent spoiled of his authority in recalling his son, but far more when he giveth his express consent. In the present case, we had the consent both of the King our father, and the Church our mother, yea they went before us in example, subscribed, and sworn the Confession aforesaid themselves. The Bishop of Elie in *Tortura Torti* answering to Matheus Tortus advising his Majesty to grant liberty of conscience hath these words, Page 81, 82. *Integrum jam hoc illi non est: nam quod cum ea qua decet reuerentia dictum volo, non semel perjurus sit, sed bis si te audiat. Qua enim (siqua est fidei bis datae conscientia) vel conscientia vel fide, ferret in regnis suis ritus vestros, vel usum eorum publicum, qui suscepta primum Scotiae, suscepta dein Angliae corona regia, utrobique solenni ritu jusjurendum Deo praestitit, de conservanda in statu suo illa colendi Dei formula, nec alia quam quae in regnis suis tum publice recepta, & utriusque gentis legibus stabilita esset. Quarum etiam se tum legum quoque, non minus quam religionis, sanctissimè in se suscepit defensorem fore? Eo autem consilium hoc tuum tendit, ut novator sit, ut periurus, ut uterque sit: esset enim uterque, si utroque hoc tam gravi crimine, vel coronae suae, vel etiam vitae securitatem redimeret.* The Bishop is bold to affirm that his Majesty cannot permit liberty of conscience, because he was twice sworn to maintain the form and manner of God's worship received and established in his kingdoms. If his Majesty may not permit another form of God's worship then that which was received already, nor the use of Papistical rites, far less in the Bishop's judgment, may his Majesty enjoin, or command other forms and rites. As for our other Superior, the Kirk, it cannot be denied but persons of all estates have subscribed and sworn since the year of God 1580. The oath and subscription was universal *Anno* 1580, 1581, 1582 & *Anno* 1590. When the general band was made for the maintenance of true Religion, and his Majesty's state and person, the said confession was published with the general band, and subscribed. So again *Anno* 1596, when the covenant was renewed in the general Assembly, in the provincial Assemblies, in Presbyteries and particular Congregations, the oath was universal. Besides the universal oaths and subscriptions, upon divers occasions, some particular persons at divers times have subscribed. So, a particular rank of persons, as for example scholars passing their degrees, since the year 1587 subscribed and swore the confession of their faith at their Laureation. In like manner, every Burgess at his admission protested before God to defend the religion then professed and authorized by the Laws, to his life's end. In like manner, particular Presbyteries, and Synods of late years: as for example, The Ministers of the Synod of Lowthian assembled at Tranent *Anno* 1604 subscribed the confession of faith. The two pretended Archbishops now living, were present and subscribed with the rest of their brethren. Any man may see, that few are excepted, who have not made their personal oath. And least any man think himself exemed [exempt], let him consider that the general Assembly, the Kirk representative made a solemn oath by holding up their hands, at the renewing of the covenant *Anno* 1596. This oath of the Kirk representative obligeth them all who were living, to the maintenance of the purity of religion in Doctrine and discipline as it was then professed. Yea the oath representative of Joshua, and the Princes of Israel representing God's people oblished [bound] their posterity: and therefore many hundred years after was the famine sent upon the land for the violation of this oath made to the Gibeoni's and Saul's seven sons were hanged. The young ones were not excepted in our oath: for the Parents did bind for them, when they were baptized, to bring them up in the confession of faith, as it was then professed in the Kirk, as grounded upon, and consonant unto the covenant of grace made betwixt God and men for themselves and for their seed. So ye see the oath of the Kirk of Scotland was partly personal and partly real. Is any Assembly, never so lawful, free, and formal, able to free us of this oath, let be a pretended Assembly, disturbed, and divided in itself, and drawing down in one session, these things which were built up in many years, and by many famous and notable Assemblies, consenting in one heart. But as I have said, our oath was with consent of the Assembly and Kirk of Scotland. Seeing we are sworn severally, how can the same persons assembled together in one body collective, dispense with this oath, seeing they have sworn to defend during their lives. To consent to any alteration, is not to defend during their lives, but rather to betray the cause, and incur perjury. If they may not violate their oath assembled collective, far less may a general assembly representing only the collective body free them of their oath, least of a null and unlawful Assembly.

    They allege they have not violated their oath, because the substance of Religion is kept, and only some indifferent points altered. But I answer. First that an oath cannot be said to be kept, unless it be kept in all the parts and contents, and in the form and manner expressed, *Nam juramentum servandum est in forma specifica*. We swore to keep the same form or worship that was used in the Kirk of Scotland, and specially in the use of the sacraments. This specification (the Kirk of Scotland) admitteth neither English, Lutheran, nor Roman rites in the worship of God different from our profession. Next our oath was in a matter of religion which is not changeable as statutes of republics and corporations are. And every point of the confession of a faith is a note of profession, whereby we profess ourselves to be distinguished either in substance, or purity of religion from others. Confessions of faith should not be changeable as Hilarius complained of his times *Annuas & menstruas fides de Deo decernimus*. Thirdly put the case, the points of our profession that are innovated were matters indifferent, as they were not so understood at the times of our oaths and subscriptions, but were declaimed against, as points of plain papistry, yet seeing indifferent things abjured for their abuse may not be received how can we receive them, except it were proved, that our oath was at the beginning unlawful; or that our former forms are become unlawful, not expedient for edification of the Kirk, or less edificative then the ceremonies presently urged. It was plainly confessed in the last pretended Assembly, that they were not expedient for our Kirk, & that they yielded to hold off an outward and external inconvenience, a matter uncertain and depending in the effect upon God's providence yea a matter now denied, as importing tyranny for so is it constantly, reported. In the mean time our assertory oath is already past, and we become perjured if we come in the contrary. This is a high degree of perjury, when not only we contravene our oath by practice, but make Laws in the contrary, and thereafter inveigh against our oath as Puritanism. If sincere and constant professors shall be still pursued for their constancy in their profession, and the conscience they make of their oath: Do we not expone [expose] the whole Nation to a woeful vengeance, and perpetual ignominy.

The unlawfulness of every one of the Articles shall be proved, as need shall require, and opportunity will serve.

KNEELING IN THE ACT
OF RECEIVING THE SACRAMENTAL
elements of Bread and Wine,
proved unlawful.

It hath been the uniform and constant order of this Kirk, since the reformation: that the communicants should receive the sacramental elements of bread and wine, sitting at the table. In the second head of the first book of discipline, are set down these words. The table of the Lord is then rightly ministered, when it approcheth most near to Christ's own action: but plain it is, that at that supper Christ Jesus sat with his disciples: and therefore we do judge that sitting at a table, is most convenient to that holy action. In the general Assembly holden in December 1562 it was ordained that one uniform order be observed in the ministration of the Sacraments, according to the order of Geneva. And in December *Anno* 1564 it was ordained that Ministers in ministration of the Sacraments, shall use the order set down in the Psalm books. In the Assembly holden anno 1591: it was ordained, That an Article should be formed, and presented to his Majesty, and the estates, craving order to be taken with them, who give or receive the sacrament after the Papistical manner. In the King's confession of faith, subscribed and sworn, by persons of all estates: are contained these words: We detest all the ceremonies of the Roman Antichrist added to the ministration of the Sacraments; we detest all his rites, signs, and traditions. This laudable order was altered at the pretended Assembly holden last at Perth in August anno 1618. The tenor of the Act followeth as it was formed by some of the Bishops, and their followers. Since we are commanded by God himself, that when we come to worship him, we fall down and kneel before the Lord our Maker: and considering withal, that there is no part of divine worship more heavenly and spiritual, then is the holy receiving of the blessed body and blood of our Lord and Saviour Jesus Christ; like as the most humble and reverend gesture of the body in our meditation, and lifting up of our hearts, best becommeth so divine and sacred an action. Therefore, notwithstanding that our Church hath used since the reformation of religion, to celebrate the holy communion to the people, sitting, by reason of the great abuse of kneeling at the worshipping of the Sacrament by the Papists, yet now seeing all memory of by past superstition is past, and no peril of the same again is feared: In reverence of so divine a mystery, and in remembrance of so mystical an union as we are made partakers of, thereby do ordain, that that blessed Sacrament be celebrated hereafter meekly and reverently upon their knees. This alteration is to us unlawful, for that which hath been established by so many laws, Civil and Ecclesiastical, by so long custom, and prescription of time, confirmed by our oaths, and subscriptions, we may not lawfully alter. But so it is, that sitting at the table in the act of receiving, hath been established by laws, custom, long prescription of time, and confirmed by oaths and subscriptions as is evident by the former deduction. It is notwithstanding expedient to descend further in opening up the unlawfulness of kneeling. 1. As it is a breach of the institution. 2. As it is a breach of the second commandment. 3. As it is with out example and practice of the ancient Kirk. 4. As it disagreeth from the practice of the reformed Kirks.

Kneeling, considered, as it is a breach of the institution.

The manner of Christ's proceeding, from the paschal supper to the Eucharistical, is to be observed, for the better understanding of the Institution. Before and in the days of Christ, the Paschal supper consisted, of two services or suppers, and a conclusion.

After the ordinary washing of their hands, they sat down to the first service, and eat the Paschal lamb with unleavened bread. Then they rose to the washing of their feet; thereafter, they sat down again to the second supper or service, and did eat of a salad, made of sour herbs, and dipped in a composed liquor, as thick as mustard. Judas after he gat a sop of this second service, he went out immediately. In the conclusion of the second service of the Paschal supper, the Lord of the house took an unleavened cake of bread and blessed it, after this manner. Blessed art thou o Lord our God, King of the World, who hast sanctified us by thy precepts, and hast given us a commandment concerning the eating of unleavened bread. Christ likewise took the bread and gave thanks. The Lord of the house, after thanks-giving break the bread, and gave it unto the company, saying, This is the bread of misery, which our fathers eat in Egypt: whosoever hungereth let him come near and eat, whosoever hath need, let him come near and celebrate the Passover. Christ after thanks-giving break the bread, and gave it to his disciples, saying, take ye, eat ye, this is my body that is broken for you. Thereafter the Lord of the house took the cup, and blessed it after this manner. Blessed art thou O Lord who hast created the fruit of the vine, after he had tasted the cup he gave it to the nearest and so it was carried from hand to hand. This cup was called, the cup of praise and thanks-giving, because they sung a Psalm after it. Christ took the cup likewise, and after he had given thanks gave it to the nearest of his disciples, saying, take ye, drink ye all of this; for this cup, is the new-testament of my blood &c. the cup was carried from hand to hand, the supper ended

50

they sung a Psalm. Morneus[1] and Beza[2] do set down this manner of proceeding, as observed before by Munsterus, Paulus Burgensis, Tremellius, Cassander, and Josephus Scaliger. Josephus Scaliger setteth down[3] a paschal canon, forbidding, to take any meat or drink after the cup of thanksgiving. This discourse being permitted the breaches of the institution are to be considered.

The first breach of the institution made by kneeling, is the taking away of that commendable gesture of sitting, used by Christ and his Apostles, at, and after the Institution. Christ and his Apostles sat at table, after the form of their usual sitting at ordinary banquets and feasts. They sat at the first service of the Paschal supper. Baradius, Swarez, Jansenius, and others affirm, that there is no circumstance in the text, *Exodus 12*, to enforce standing at the Passover. Next, suppose the circumstances there expressed did import standing, yet it was not enjoined as an ordinary rite, but as many other circumstances, belonged only to the first Passover in Egypt, as to eat with haste, and with loins girded up, and to sprinkle the lintel and two side posts of the door with blood, as Beza hath observed[4] and Scaliger in the late edition of his books *de emendatione temporum*[5] saith the like: put the case, that this gesture continued longer, yet long before the days of Christ this gesture was changed. Scaliger produceth out of the rituals of the Jews,[6] their words: *Quam diversa haec nox à ceteris noctibus quod in aliijs noctibus semel tantum levamus in hac autem bis. Quod in reliquis noctibus comedimus sive fermentum sive Azimum in hac autem onmino azyma. Quod in reliquis noctibus vescimur oleribus omne genus in hoc autem intybis. Quod in omnibus noctibus tam edentes quam bibentes vel sedemus vel*

---

[1] *lib. 1. de missa cap. 1*
[2] In Met c. 26:20
[3] de emendat. temporum. lib. 6
[4] Annot. in Mat. 26:20
[5] Lib. 6. p. 534
[6] De emendat. temp. lib. 6. p. 539

discumbimus in hac autem omnes discumbimus. How far different is this night from other nights? Other nights we wash once, this night twice: other nights we eat leavened or unleavened bread, this night only unleavened. Other nights we eat all sorts of herbs, this night only Chicory. Other nights as well eating as drinking, we either sit or sup; this night we all sup, that is, sit leaning. In his first Edition he saith, that the book *Kiddush Pesach*, out of which their words are alleged, is a little elder then Christ's time. It is clear then, that *Anakeimenon discumbentibus*, cannot be translated, standing, neither did ever any translator so translate the word anywhere. It is said likewise, they sat down at the second service after he had washen the disciples' feet. And whilst they did eat, *edentibus illis, Mathew 26:26 & Mark 14:22*, Christ took bread and blessed, &c. If whilst they did eat, then also whilst they did sit. As these two are conjoined, *Mark 14:18*. The phrase imports, that nothing intervened betwixt the eating and the celebration of the sacrament: it was ministered therefore unto them sitting. This is so evident that never man doubted of it till this last year. Even these who affirm but against the truth, that they stood at the first service, confess that they sat at the second, and the celebration of the Sacrament. M. John Mare in *Mathew 26* saith,[1] That Christ sat, and he brings in an old verse to this effect: *Rex sedet in coena, turba cinctus duodena. Se tenet in manibus, se cibat ipse cibus.* The Bishop of Chester[2] confesseth, That it is true, Christ did administer the sacrament in a kind of sitting gesture, and that in the same gesture the Apostles did receive it.

That sitting was institute[d], I prove it by two reasons. First, the gesture that Christ retained in passing from the conclusion of the Paschal Supper, that he did institute: sitting he retained, therefore sitting he did institute. In the conclusion of the Paschal Supper some things were changed, other things

---

[1] *Tametsi agnum typinum dominus tans comederit ritu legis, sedens samen communicavit.*
[2] Desence pag. 248

were retained, a third sort were neither changed, nor retained as belonging to the institution, but only of occasional necessity which could not conveniently be changed, but were done necessarily: as for example, unleavened bread because there was no other, the circumstance of the time, the parlor and such other circumstances belonging to the Passover, they were retained of necessity, by reason of the present occasion of the Paschal Supper and could not conveniently have been changed. But as for the gesture of sitting, he might have changed it, in standing, or kneeling without working any miracle, if it had not been his mind that we should receive the sacrament of the Eucharistical Supper, with the same gesture the Jews received the Paschal Supper. The second reason, we are bound to imitate Christ, and the commendable example of his Apostles, in all things wherein it is not evident, that they had special reasons moving them thereto which do not concern us. Yea it is gross hypocrisy for us, to pretend more reverence and devotion in the act of receiving, then the Apostles did when Christ was present, or the Apostolic Kirks did lately after the Institution. Wherefore doth the Apostle propone the custom of the first Kirks. *1 Corinthians 11:16 & 14:33, 2 Tim. 3:14.* If they did not oblige us to imitation? When Christ was in the state of humility they sat: he was worshiped upon extraordinary occasions. *Mathew 9:18* and *8:2* and *14:33* and *20:20, John 9:38*, they were not now in any common action, or at an ordinary Supper, they had now reason to kneel if they should have kneeled at all. After his resurrection, when he was in Emmaus with some of the disciples, it is said *Luke 24:30*, that as he sat at meat with them, he took bread, blessed it, brake it, and gave it unto them. This place is interpret of the Sacrament by Augustine, Paulinus, Esychius, Theophilactus, Beda, Euthimius, Hieronimus, all alleged by Bellarmin[1] and Gregorius de Valentia[2]: they allege also some of our own writers to the same purpose but so it is, they were

---

[1] De Eucharist. l. 4. c. 24
[2] De legitimousu Eucharist. cap. 7

sitting when Christ gave them the bread, whatsoever be the interpretation of the text, ye see they acknowledge sitting at table. Last of all, after his ascension and glorification in the heavens, the Apostolic Kirk sat at table. The manner of the partaking of the table of devils was by formal sitting at table in the house of the Idol:[1] Jonathan the Chaldee paraphrased *Amos 2:8*, interpreteth the garments whereon the usurer sat beside every Altar, to have been beds prepared in the houses of their gods, to sit on when they feasted upon things sacrificed to Idols. The people of Israel sat down to eat and drink at the Idolatrous feast of the golden calf. The Apostle compareth the partaking of the Lord's table, and the table of devils, *1 Corinthians 10:21*. Next, they sat at the love feasts: we cannot think that they rose from the tables, either before or after the love feasts, to receive the Sacrament severally out of Paul's hand. Bilson saith, they sat at table[2] and to this purpose allegeth Augustine:[3] *Non debent fratres mensis suis ista miscere sicut faciebant quos Apostolus arguit & emendat*, we may se then Christ instituted it, the Apostolic Kirks followed it, no different respect of the state of Christ's humility or glory brought in any other gesture.

It is objected that the sitting of Christ and his Apostles was not upright but sitting with leaning. If we imitate the example of Christ, we should sit after the same manner.

Answer. It was the custom received amongst the Jews before and in the days of Christ, descending from the Romans, or as others allege from the Persians, *Esther 1*. The table was situate in the midst of the hall or parlor, and the beds about the table except the part that was free for the service of the table: They sat upon the beds somewhat leaning toward the table and their feet lying out at the out-side of the beds. The beds of the rich and wealthy were so high, that it behooved them to ascend by steps. There was a space

---

[1] 1 Cor. 8:10
[2] Obedience p. 460
[3] Epist. 11

between the beds and the walls of the Hall or Parlor, that servants might have room to stand at the feet of the guests, and make service. They that stood behind to serve, were said, *stare à pedibus*, to stand at their feet, as Petrus Ciacconius proveth out of Seneca and Suetonius.[1] By this discourse we may understand, first, that when Mary stood at Christ's feet, *Luke 7:38* she lay not groveling at his feet,[2] as the Bishop of Rochester perverteth the gesture. Next, that Christ and his Apostles used at supper the gesture used at ordinary suppers. If we sit therefore according to the received gesture of the Country wherein we are, we imitate aright, and it were apeth imitation to sit otherwise. It is indifferent whether we use white or red wine we are no more bound to the wine of Judea, then to the wine of France, at the ministration of the Supper: these are but national differences. Thirdly, there is so little difference betwixt the one fashion of sitting and the other, that both the words, *diseumbers* and *sedere* are translated indifferently, to sit, in the English translations. The delicate and sinful woman, *Ezekiel 23* is said to sit in a glorious bed, and a table spread before her. Josephus translateth the sitting of Joseph's brethren by the word *Kataclinein*, signifying, half sitting, half leaning, howbeit upright sitting was the gesture used in Joseph's time, a man standing leaning, is said to stand as well as when he stands upright, siclyk [likewise] sitting. Leaning is a position of the body common to sitting or standing. The Jews themselves at this day sit upright at their Paschal supper.

There is a difference betwixt customs brought into the Kirk by invention of men, and the custom brought in by Christ, and entertained by his Apostles; as there is a difference betwixt the Lord's Day and the Holy days invented by men. It is safer for mans conscience to imitate Christ and his Apostles, then to depart from them, and imitate the custom of Kirks, which may err. Yea, Christ's example seconded with the

---

[1] *De Triclivio*
[2] *Discourse of Kneeling* p. 1351

practice of the Apostles, is equivalent to a precept as I have said. Yea this gesture may very well be comprehended under the express precept of Christ in the institution, *Hoc facite*, do this: that is, *hoc totum facite*, do all this. For we must not think that nothing belongeth to the institution, but that which is mentioned in Paul's narration, *1 Corinthians 11* for then a table should not belong to the institution: no doubt our Saviour instructed them how to discern the Lord's body, how to eat and drink, before he commanded them to eat and drink. But the Evangelists, and Paul writes of the Sacrament as of a thing known to the Kirk by practice, presupposing a table, and the communicants convened and sitting at the table.

The second breach of the Institution made by kneeling in the act of receiving, is the taking away of the use of a table. Christ and his Apostles sat at table, *1 Corinthians 10 & Luke 22* wherefore serves the name of a table if we keep not the proper use and employment of it? The fathers call it the Lord's table, the heavenly table, the sacred table, the mystical table, the spiritual table, the rational table: whereto serve all these commendations, if in the mean time it be not used as a table, but rather as an altar? If it be not used as Christ and his Apostles used it, that is by sitting at it to receive of the dainties set upon the table? The Sacrament is called a Supper and therefore a table is answerable to it. It is never termed a Sacrifice in the Scripture. We sit at tables, but not at altars: we eat and drink at tables, but not all altars. The ancients called this table an altar, but unproperly & in respect of the commemoration of Christ's sacrifice. This improper speech was dangerous, & has proven hurtful to the Kirk transforming indeed a table into an Altar. If we retain no more but the name of a table, the Papists can, and do give that name to the lid of their Altar. The people of God had an altar for the sacrifice, and a table for a feast. Siclyk [likewise] the Ethnicks [pagans]. So Christians have one altar for one sacrifice, to wit, Christ who is Priest, Altar, and Sacrifice, *Hebrews 13:10* and a table for the feast after this sacrifice once made, to wit, the

Sacrament of the Supper. As the Israelites and the Ethniks sat at the tables of their feasts made of things sacrificed, so do we at our sacred feasts, to distinguish between an Altar and a table, a sacrifice and a Supper made of the thing sacrificed. A dresser or Cupboard may serve as well for disposing of the elements, and reaching them to the communicants as a table. If a table should serve, to no other use but to set on these Elements, and reach them from the table; Christ and his Apostles used not the table after that manner. As it served them to the Paschal Supper, so it served to the Eucharistical.

The third breach of the institution made by kneeling, is the taking away of that mystical rite representing Christ's passion, to wit, the breaking of the bread. The Apostle says not, The communion of one bread; but, The communion of one broken bread hath in it a mystery of our unity. When the bread is carved in little morsels before it be presented to the table, it is not the sacramental and mystical breaking in the use of the Sacrament which ought to be performed after the thanksgiving according to Christ's example. Augustine saith: *Cum illud quod est in Domini mensa benedicitur & sanctificatur,*[1] *& ad distribuendum comminuitur.* When that which is blessed on the Lord's table, sanctified, and broken in small pieces to be distributed, &c. This breaking was needful both for mystery and distribution. The breaking of the bread was thought so needful in the Sacrament, that it was called, Breaking of Bread. The Syriac interpreter translateth the breaking of bread Eucharist, *Acts 2:24* and *20:7*. Pareus on *1 Corinthians 11* proveth at length this rite not to be indifferent, but a thing commanded. Where kneeling is practiced, we read not in their Service-books of this breaking of bread after thanksgiving: whereby the passion of Christ is not set forth to the communicants as it ought to be.

The fourth breach of the institution made by kneeling, is the change and restraint of the commandment given to many

---

[1] Epist. 59. *ad Paulinum.*

in the plural number, Eat ye, drink ye: to one in the singular number, Eat thou, drink thou. Fenner in the doctrine of the sacraments, expresseth the pith of this phrase in a lively manner. It is fittest (saith he) to note out the fellowship and communion of the Church in this work, the person of Christ by the Minister, bidding all his guests with one love as from him to be merry, and eat with faith one spiritual meat together. Our faith is further succored, when we may together, and with one heart, apply ourselves to the meditation and fruit of this speech of Christ by the Minister, which in the particular speaking doth loose that our working together, and maketh the minds of Christians hang the longer in the waiting for this sentence, and the comfort of it, and their minds are offered unto greater occasions of slips and with drawings, by human infirmity, when these things are prolonged, which may more effectually be done together and speedily.

The fifth breach of the institution made by kneeling, is, the altering of the enunciative words of Christ, This is my body which is broken for you: whereby he declares his coming in the flesh and suffering for sin, the main ground of our redemption, and, changing them in a prayer to bless our body and soul. The body of our Lord Jesus Christ which was given for thee, preserve thy body and soul unto everlasting life. The Papist in this point goeth nearer to the institution: for he giveth not the Eucharist, except the host be first consecrated at some Mass, with these words, This is my body. This prayer inserted betwixt the thanksgiving and the distribution, and repeated to every communicant, is idle battology [repetition]. The use of the prayer and thanksgiving for the use of the elements, endureth all the time of the action. Christ's words in the institution contain partly a command, partly a promise, partly institution. Christ's promise is contained in their definitive words, This is my body that is given for you: This is my blood which is shed for the remission of the sins of many. When the form of the words is altered, the promise is obscured. It is not enough to rehearse the words of the institution in the prayer immediately preceding the action, but in the action every rite and ceremony should have the words of the institution concurring. Let the word be joined with the element, and so it shall be a sacrament, saith Augustine.

The sixth breach of the institution made by kneeling, is the taking away of the distribution that ought to be amongst the communicants. When Christ said, Take ye, eat ye, he insinuates that they should take and divide amongst themselves. The word *Edoke*, he gave, doth not import that he gave immediately. The Disciples in setting the bread before the five thousand, *Mark 6:41* gave the bread to the five thousand, *Matthew 14:19* the five thousand distributed among themselves. Cajetanus upon *Matthew 26* acknowledgeth, that the Disciples were in so great distance from Christ, that their hands could not meet with his hands, Beza saith,[1] that howbeit Christ had sitten in the midst, as Painters make him to sit, yet in respect of the manner of their sitting, it behooved either Christ to rise and come to them that were far distant, or them to come to him, if he had given the elements to every one in their own hands. Tossaus saith, that Christ gave to the two nearest,[2] and they reached to them who were further off. In the first book of Discipline penned *Anno* 1560 it is ordained that the Minister break the bread, and distribute the same to those that be next him, commanding the rest every one with reverence and sobriety to break with other, because it is nearest to Christ's action. Further, we have a plain precept, *Luke 22:17*. Divide it amongst you, speaking of the communion Cup, and not of the Paschal. The Evangelists make mention of four things belonging to the communion cup. 1. Thanksgiving. 2. Distribution. 3. Assertion that it is his blood. 4. A protestation that he will not drink of the Vine until the kingdom of God shall come: the assertion that it is his

---

[1] Epist. 2
[2] In Mat. 26

blood, is set down afterward by *Luke 22:20* the other 3 are set down in this 17th verse. It is therefore the same cup. Next, if it had not been the communion cup, and consequently the last, the communion cup behooved to have come after: but that cannot agree with the protestation: for how could Christ protest of the Paschal cup that he would drink no more of the fruit of the wine, if he drank after it of the Evangelical cup. The paschal canon interdicted to eat or drink after the cup of thanksgiving or praise, the cup of praise in the end of the paschal Supper was changed as I have said into the Eucharistical cup, & was all one with it: and the protestation of not drinking, more agreeth with the Canon made of the last Paschal cup all one with the Evangelical. This cup was carried about from hand to hand, and divided amongst them by themselves. The two Evangelists do not so much as mention the cup of the Passover and yet make mention of this protestation of not drinking more of the fruit of the Vine. The verses immediately proceeding the protestation, make mention only of the cup of the Lord's Supper, *Matthew 26:28 & Mark 14:24*. Fulk saith, the demonstrative pronoun (this) *Matthew 26:29* declareth, that he spake of the wine in his hand that is of the communion cup. If there was two cups then either the words of the protestation were repeated, or set down by Matthew and Mark out of the one place, and wrongfully applied, but none of these two is to be admitted. Thirdly, Luke omitteth the mention of thanksgiving and the commandment to drink of this cup, verse 20, howbeit both be expressly set down by other Evangelists, and the analogy with the actions concerning the bread requireth the same. Wherefore then did he omit them? Even because speaking before of the same cup, verse 17, he had made mention of these two points, he escheweth to repeat them as already mentioned. And wherefore made he mention of the cup, verse 17, even that the protestation of not drinking more, verse 17, might be joined with the protestation of not eating more, verse 16, he maketh mention of the assertion of his blood, verse 20, because it was not yet spoken of. The other 3 points are omitted as already spoken of, verse 17, this inversion of order and making mention of the cup of the communion before the order of Institution, was observed long since be[1] Augustine and[2] Euthymius, and is acknowledged not only by our own divines, but also by Barradius, Jansenius, and other learned papists, Theobaldus Meushius[3] observeth a constant continual inversion of the order in this chapter of Luke. *Operae pretium est in his advertere hysteron proteron Lucae contrarium.* Augustine saith, *anti ipavit ut sotet.* There is a clear instance, verse 21, after the words of the Institution it is said, Behold the hand of him that betrayeth me, is with me at the table. Now it is clear, that Judas went out immediately after he received the sop. Zacharias[4] Chrisopolitanus observed herein a recapitulation of some things pretermitted [omitted] before. *Quod post calicem datum, traditorem commemorat pretermissa recapitulare videtur.* Beza in his annotations conjectureth, that the verses are transposed, and that the 19th and 20th verses should be subjoined to the 16th, and that the 17th verse should be subjoined to the 19th and 20th. Bilson[5] and Jewel[6] against Harding and many other divines, disputing against the private masse, exponeth the words, *Luke 22:17* divide it amongst you, of the communion cup. That wich is spoken of the cup should be meant also of the bread, for as Christ said, Take ye, drink ye, so said he, Take ye, eat ye. Tyndale[7] in his tractate of restoring the Lord's Supper, requireth that every man break & reach forth to his neighbor. This distribution amongst the communicants was commanded, no doubt to nourish love, and to be a bond of

---

[1] *Lib. 3. de consensu Evang.*
[2] In Mat. 26
[3] *Desensio harmoniae generalis*
[4] Harmon. Evang. lib. 4 cap. 156.
[5] Obedience pag. 495.
[6] Of privat Masse, division 8.
[7] Pag. 477

union amongst the communicants and agreeth best with the nature of a feast, where signs and tokens of amity are interchanged. Clemens Alexandrinus[1] saith it was permitted to every one of the people, to take a part of the Eucharist. *Etiam Eucharistiam cum quidam ut mos est diuiserint, permittitur uni uique ex populo partem ejus sumere.* When Tertullim saith, *We receive it of no other hands, but the hands of our presidents, or rulers,* he meaneth not simply of pastors but of any governors Ecclesiastical whatsoever. And suppose he mean only of pastors, yet he confesseth it to be tradition and no scripture, as Junius hath observed upon that place. Howsoever this was the custom in Africa to receive it out of the minister's hand, yet not so at Rome and every where: for Justinus[2] telleth us how the Deacons gave to every one of them that were present, part of the bread and likewise of the wine.

In the liturgy of St. James, it is said that the Deacons lift up the dishes and cups to impart to the people. It came to pass afterward that the Deacons dispensed not the bread, but the wine only, the ridiculous reasons whereof are set down by Aquinas[3] this superstitious custom, of taking it out of the Minister's hand, did grow afterward to Superstitious receiving in at the mouth, and in some parts to the drawing of the wine out of the cups with silver pipes, the minister ought not, howbeit he might commodiously, give the elements out of his own hand to every communicant, because it is against the institution and purpose of Christ, willing the communicants by this rite, to entertain communion amongst themselves. Whatsoever action or command is enclosed within the institution, may not lawfully be broken: but that the communicants should distribute amongst themselves, was both an action at the first supper, and a precept, as I have proven. This precept and action by consequence dischargeth

---

[1] Stromat. lib. 1
[2] Apol. 2
[3] Part. 3. quaestr 82. art. 3

kneeling, because that gesture and this distribution is no ways compatible.

Christ's general precept, *do this* maketh the actions of the first supper precepts. The particular precept *divide it amongst you* leaveth no place to any tergiversation.

The seventh breach of the institution made by kneeling is, an unnecessary dividing of the communicants, making populous congregations to receive on many days where they may receive in one. Every particular congregation ought to be convened *Epi to auto* into one place, at one time to communicate together as far as is possible. Although all the faithful communicate with Christ's body spiritually, yet they only communicate Sacramentaly, who have their communion sealed by the outward action of eating of one Sacramental bread it being a commandment of the Apostle, that every one should tarry one upon an other when they assemble themselves to celebrate the holy Supper, it followeth that they should receive together, Ambrose expounding these words, saith, *Expectandum dicit ut multorum oblatio simul celebretur et omnibus ministretur*, they must tarry that the oblation of many may be celebrate together, and so be ministered to them all. Leo writing to Diosiorus, gave him this advice, that where the Church was so little, that it was not able to receive all the people to communicate together, the Priest should minister two or three communions in one day. Calixtus[1] ordained, that consecration ended, all communicate, that will not stand excommunicate, for so the Apostle determined, and the holy Roman Kirk observeth. See more of this purpose in Jewel's sermon at Paul's Crosse.

The eight breach of the institution made by kneeling is, the altering of the purpose of the institution, or nature of this Sacrament. It was instituted to be a supper, a spiritual feast: it was the will of Christ therefore, that we should behave ourselves as guests invited to a banquet. Guests invited to a

---

[1] De consecrat. dist, 2. Peracta

banquet, even to a Prince's banquet kneel not in the act of banqueting. They are invited indeed to a spiritual refreshment, but the Sacramental Supper should carry the resemblance of a supper, in the forms and fashions thereof, or else it could not rightly be called a Supper; for it is not only the matter, that is, the dainties and food, that maketh a banquet, but also the ordering of the guests, and kindly entertainment of them. The Sacrament of the Passover was also a holy Supper, and the people of God used it so: they kneeled not in the act of receiving of it. When they received the law of the Passover, they bowed the heads and worshipped, *Exodus 12:27*. Yet did they not so in the eating of it. They were more reverent and devout, in hearing the law of it out of the mouth of Moses then in the participation of it.

Let no man object against us, the examples of some kirks, where some of the former breaches are made without kneeling: seeing kneeling hath made them all, and seeing we have the institution, standing to us in force of a command, wherein nothing should be altered, in matter, form, or order; nothing added; nothing diminished: for divine institutions admit, neither addition nor diminution[1] the Apostle allegeth the institution against all abuses, *that which I received of the Lord, that have I delivered unto you, 1 Corinthians 11:23*. Doubtless (saith Pareus) *he received this history of the institution from the Lord, with other revelations, when he was ravished to the third heavens*. It is not my invention (would the Apostle say) but the Lord's ordinance, concredit [entrusted] unto me to be kept as a jewel. It is not for naught, that the Evangelists with one consent do set down the form of this institution, and that the Apostle trieth all corruptions in the Supper by it, as by a rule. Ciprian saith *Epist, 3. lib. 3* we must follow the truth of God, and not the custom of men. And in another place he saith when the channels are corrupted we should run to the

---

[1] Saith Pareus in 1 Cor. 11

fountain. It is not so much our purpose to tax others as to defend ourselves.

Kneeling considered, as it is a breach of the second commandment.

Kneeling in the act of receiving the Sacramental elements, is not only a breach of the institution in the Gospel, but also of the second commandment of the law.

The first breach of the commandment made by kneeling is, the sin of Idolatry. Idolatry is committed in this act divers ways. The Papists kneel in the act of receiving, because they believe verily, that the bread is transubstantiate into Christ's body, and upon this supposition of transubstantiation and bodily presence, they kneel. This is the grossest idolatry that ever was in the world. The Lutheran kneeleth upon his supposition of consubstantiation, and Christ's real presence by consubstantiation: this also is idolatry and the supposition false. A third sort kneel for reverence of the Elements, not giving to the Elements that high kind of worship called commonly *cultus latriae*, which the Papist giveth, but an inferior kind of worship due (as they think) to consecrate creatures: this also is Idolatry.

Kneeling for reverence of the elements, is Idolatry, because it is a religious worship of a creature. It is not civil worship they give in the act of receiving the sacred Elements: the matter and motive of their reverence is a matter of religion, to wit, because the elements are holy signs and seals: it is therefore religious worship. Religious worship is divine worship. All manner of worship pertaining to godliness and religion, is religious worship.[1] Divine or godly worship is all manner of worship pertaining to godliness and religion (saith Doctor Abbots.) Divine worship is proper to God: therefore religious worship, or worship of religion is peculiar to God

---
[1] Defence of Perkins 2. part. pag. 1180

alone. Augustine saith: *Apostolus & creaturam laudat & citamen cultus religionis exhibere vetat.*[1] The Apostle commendeth the creature, forbiddeth nevertheless that worship of religion be yielded to it. And again he saith,[2] *Quis dicat non debere observare Christianos ut uni Deo religionis obsequium serviatur*: Christians are to observe that with the duty of religion they serve God only. Peter and the Angel refused religious worship. If it may not be given to Angels and Saints, far less may it be given to dead elements and senseless creatures. To kneel for reverence of the elements, and a religions estimation of them in the mind, is to determine adoration in the creature. Some honor redoundeth to God, or Christ, but that convoy by redundance, is common to all respective, and dependant worships given to dead and senseless things: for Creatures without sense are not worshipped absolutely for holiness, virtue, or any other excellency inherent in themselves, but for their conjunction with, or representation of the persons represented, in whom the excellency is intrinsically: and this the Papist will grant, not only of his Images, but of all sacred things also. They are worshipped only in respect of the person, yet notwithstanding of this dependant and respective worship, they affirm the sacred things are worshipped *per se*, howbeit, not *propter se*, by themselves, howbeit not for themselves; because by themselves they have relation, or conjunction with or representation of the persons adored: that is, they have in them a cause of adoration, howbeit a dependent cause. Swarez saith, *Honor illis exhilitus non in illis sistit,*[3] *sed in ipsas personas propter quas adorantur, redundat.* That the honor determined in the Images or sacred things, redoundeth notwithstanding to the principle. He that honoreth a man's image, honoreth it for his sake whose image it is. This transient worship is convoyed to the principle, only mediately: God will have no mediate creature to go between

---

[1] Contra Faust. lib. 14 c. 11
[2] Contra 2. epist. Pelag. lib. 3. cap. 4
[3] In Aquinatem. Tom. 1. Disput 51 sect. 3

him and his worship: he will not communicate a glance of this worship to any creature. Civil worship is convoyed mediately to the person of the Prince, by bowing to senseless creatures, as to the chair of Estate, the cloth of Estate, the King's letter and seal, because the estate thinks it expedient for Princely Majesty that these things be reverenced, which serve in a special manner for the Prince's use, as signs of his presence or pleasure. But the ceremonies of the Court, and mediate civil worships, are not rules of religious adoration. For as Augustine saith, *Multa de cultu divino usurpata sunt, quae honoribus deferuntur humanis,*[1] *sive humilitate nimi, sive adulatione pestisera.* That too great humility or pestiferous flattery, may be the original of many human honors and courtesies. God does inhibit mediate religious worships.

It may be objected, that holy things ought to be reverenced.

Answer. True, but not worshiped. Veneration is one thing, Adoration another. Adoration belongeth to persons. Veneration to things pertaining to persons, and is nothing else, but a religious respect, or reverent estimation of things pertaining to the use of religion, a preservation of them that they be not lost; a decently usage of them according to their kind. This veneration or reverence, is a respective or relative reverence given them for God's sake. Kneeling for reverence of senseless creatures, is, to take the proper gesture of relative adoration, and apply it to relative reverence. For religious kneeling in all the Scripture is a gesture of adoration, and sovereign worship. Augustine, speaking of the brazen serpent, sacred writings, and the bread in the Sacrament, saith.[2] *honorem tanquam religiosa habere possunt, stuporem tanquam missa non possunt.* They may have honor as matters religious, but wonder, as matters of marvel they cannot have. When Ezra read the book of the law, *Nehemiah 8:3-5* the people stood up, but when he praised God they bowed themselves and worshiped the Lord with their faces toward

---

[1] Lib. de civ. Dei. lib, 10. cap. 4
[2] De trinit. lib. 3. c. 10

the ground. Here ye see veneration and adoration, submission, and recognition of some other thing more excellent. The altar, the offerings, the Priest's garment, were holy, yet the Jews worshiped them not. The uncovering of the head, is a gesture of reverence, and yet the Gentiles had their heads covered when they worshiped their gods, as Brissonius proveth.[1] Drusius proveth the like[2] of the Jews, that they covered their head when they prayed to God. But kneeling was ever holden among all nations for a proper gesture of adoration, either civil or religious.

The Ministers of Lincolne in the third part of their defense laid to the charge of their Church representative, that kneeling is intended for reverence of the elements. I refer the reader to their proofs: for the present let it only be observed, upon what occasion kneeling was urged. In their first reformation it was left free. Gardiner, Boner, and other Papists sought to make the first Book of Common Prayer odious, amongst other things for want of reverence to the Sacrament. The Papists made insurrection, and challenged proudly in their Articles a reformation, for reverence of the Sacrament: and on the other side, some, inconsiderately fixed railing libels at Paul's-cross, and other places, terming the Sacrament lack of the box, the Sacrament of the Halter, round Roben &c. These proceedings moved Ridly in his preachings at Paul's-Crosse to proceed so far, that the chiefest papists seemed to desire no more, but that his practice might be answerable to his doctrine. This stir made also Cranmer, and Ridly, at the second reviewing of the book of common prayer, to enjoin kneeling, with this reason; that the Sacrament might not be profaned, but holden in a holy and reverent estimation. They feared to offend superstitious people in a time of strong opposition, until they were better taught, neither was their judgment clear in this cause: for they thought it not idolatry to worship the consecrate elements, with an inferior kind of worship, and for

---

[1] Formulae lib. 1
[2] Preterita. 1 Cor. 1:4

the relation they have to the thing signified, providing they yield not unto them sovereign or godly worship, as they called it. They were but newly come forth out of the dark den of popery, and could not see all things in the first dawning of the day.

In the late act, we are ordained, to kneel for reverence of the divine mysteries. I see not wherein this differeth from the Bishop of Rochester's argument,[1] that great and reverent dreadful mysteries, must be received with great and dreadful humility of soul, and humiliation of body: therefore in the act of receiving we must kneel. If this argument were good, then the Sacraments and sacrifices of the old law should have been thus worshipped: And if we will measure by the sight, the sacraments and sacrifices of the old Law were more dreadful then the sacraments of the new, for the slaughter of beasts, and Shedding of blood, was more dreadful, then the pouring out of wine. The ancients held the sight of this Sacrament, not only from pagans, but also from the Catechumenists, they preached darkly, they wrote darkly, to the same end. This doing was not commendable, it made the mystery of this Sacrament both dark and dreadful. Augustine has already said, they may be honored as matters religious but wondered at as matters of marvel they cannot. But to return to the purpose, to kneel for reverence of the mysteries is nothing else but to worship the mysteries.

Wheresoever the public intent of a Kirk is to worship the Sacrament, every private man following that intent, is formally an Idolater. If his private intent be divers from the public, yet he is still materially, & Interpretative an Idolater. If a man receive the Eucharist in the papistical Kirk on his knees, howbeit he kneel not upon the supposed conceit of transubstantiation, but his own private intent, he is materially guilty of their gross Idolatry. Ismenias stooping down before the King of Persia to take up a ring, which he let purposely

---

[1] Discourse of Kneeling pag. 124

fall, was not excused because this stooping in common use, was the adoring of the King of Persia.

Kneeling directed to the bread and wine in the hands of the Minister, is idolatry, howbeit the inward motion of the mind and affection of the hart be directed only to God, or his Son Christ, as the only object of adoration. This immediate convoy of worship to the principal object, is nothing else but that finer sort of Idolatry and relative worship, which Durandus, Holcot, Mirandula, Alphonsus, Petrus Cluniacensis, and others, give to their images. They say Images are not otherwise adored, then that before them and about them, are exhibit the external signs of honor: the inward affection is directed only to the principal object: as the services done at a funeral explain, to one empty coffin, as if the corps were present. See Bellarmine[1] and Swarez[2] when it is said therefore to varnish this second intent that the elements are not *Objectum quod*, the thing itself that is worshiped, nor *objectum in quo*, or, *per quod*, in the which, or by the which, but *objectum a quo significativè* the object or sign moving us upon the sight thereof, to lift up our hearts to the spiritual object of faith. This kind of relative worship will not be found different from the relative worship of Durandus and the rest: For Bellarmine and Swarez draw Durandus and the rest from *In illa, et per illam Imaginem*, in and by the image, to *Circum* and *Coram*, about, or before the Image. Swarez saith[3] that the image is neither the formal, nor the material, the total, nor the partial object of adoration in their opinion; but that only at the presence of the images the principal called to remembrance by the image is adored, that the image is an occasion, amidst, a sign stirring up a man to adore the principal. Their adoration then was also abstract from the object, as they pretend theirs to be. The bread and wine or any other creature whatsoever, differeth not in this present case, for howsoever they were ordained of

---

[1] De iimaginibus cap. 20
[2] In Aquin. Tom. 1. disp. 54. sect. 3
[3] Ibid. disput. 53. sect. disp. 54. sect. 4

God to be signs and seals of his graces, yet they are not *in statu accommodato ad adorandum*; they have no such state in the service of God, as that by them, or before them God or his son Christ should be adored. Next, if this kind of relative worship were to be allowed, then all the holy signs both in the old and New Testament should have served to the same use. Then they who are far distant from the table should kneel, for the Elements are to them, *objectum a quo significatiuè*. Then at the sight of the sun or any beautiful creature, we should kneel seeing they put us in mind of God's incomprehensible beauty. And seeing many of them do allow the historical use of images, we may fall down before the Crucifix, providing the action of the mind be abstracted from the image. Thirdly, all the parts of God's worship ought to be direct, and not oblique. Perkins[1] saith, it is idolatry to turn, dispose, or direct the worship of God, or any part thereof to any particular place or creature, without the appointment of God, and more specially, to direct our adoration to the bread or the place where the bread is, what is it less then Idolatry.

Kneeling before the elements referred directly to Christ is, either a gesture signifying the humble submission of the mind in general, whereby we make obeisance, as if he were bodily present: or else it signifieth more particularly our humiliation In prayer: this is but a special, the former was a general; the like reasons serve against both. It is true we cannot kneel to God in prayer, but there are many things before us, a Kirk, a house, a wall, a tree, a star, &c. But we set them not before us purposely; we are by no direction tied unto them, they stand only before us by casual position, neither can we choose otherwise to do. It is true, likewise, that God directed his people under the Law to bend and bow themselves toward the Ark, and the Temple wherein the Ark was, and the Mountain whereon the Temple was situate: partly least that rude people should turn their worship another way; partly

---

[1] Idolatry p. 677,678

because of his promise to hear them when they should pray toward the Temple, or the Ark; partly because of his singular manner of presence in the Ark: he was said to dwell between the Cherubims, the Ark is called his foot-stool? And sometime the face of God; the glory of the Lord. It is reason, where God is present after an extraordinary manner, as when he spake out of the bush, and the cloud, that adoration be directed to the place of his extraordinary presence. The Altars; the offerings and other holy things wanted the like presence, and the like promise. The Ark and the Cherubims upon the Ark, were not seen: and therefore could not be readily abused to idolatry.

The Sacramental elements have neither the like presence, the like promise, nor the like commandment. Worship is tied no longer to any certain thing or place on earth, *John 4:21, 22*. Adoration is tied in the New Testament to the manhood of Christ, the true Ark and propitiatory: and is carried to that place, in which we certainly know the said manhood to exist substantially saith Perkins,[1] and therefore it is, that we lift up our eyes to the heavens, where he is, and direct our very external worship unto him.

It is objected, and said, that we may pray in the act of receiving; therefore we may kneel in the act of receiving. *Answer*. This objection insinuates that kneeling is the proper and only commendable gesture of prayer, and therefore the Bishop of Rochester exponeth the standing of the publican, *Luke 18:11, 13* to have been kneeling, because (saith he) the Jewish custom was to pray kneeling. But if he had remembered the Lord's own saying, *Jeremiah 15* though Moses and Samuel stood before me &c. he might have understood that they prayed standing as well as kneeling. Drusius observeth,[2] that of old they prayed standing, that therefore prayers were called stations, or standings. And Rabbi Juda had a saying, that the world could not subsist without stations

---

[1] Idolatry pag. 677, 678, 700, 701
[2] In Matthew 6

or standings[1] and where it is said, Abram stood before the Lord: Manabem, an Hebrew Rabbin expoundeth it, he prayed before the Lord. Next the prayer meant of, is either some public prayer uttered by the Minister, or the mental prayer of the communicant. As for the prayer of the Minister in the act of distribution, it is flat against the institution, as I have already said. The Minister is ordained by the institution to act the person of Christ, and pronounce the words of promise. This is my body: as if Christ himself were pronouncing these words, and not change the promise into a prayer. Fenner in his principles of Religion[2] layeth this down as a ground, That in the second commandment we are forbidden the practice and use of any other rite, or outward means used in the worship or service of God, then he hath ordained, *John 4:22, 2 Kings 18:4* and that by the contrary we are commanded to practice all those parts of his worship, which he in his word hath commanded, and to acknowledge only the proper use of every rite and outward means which the Lord hath ordained. *Deuteronomy 12:32, 2 Kings 17:26*. Further, we are forbidden by the second commandment to pray by direction before any creature, This public prayer is but a pretended cause of kneeling, as the Ministers of Lincolne make manifest in their abridgement: for no Canon of our neighbor Kirk hath directed any part of this kneeling in the act of receiving, to be assigned to the said prayer. In populous congregations, where there is but one Minister, the communicants sit a quarter of an hour before the Minister repair to them with the sacrament. And last, the prayer is ended before the delivery of the elements. As for our Kirk, no such prayer is ordained to be uttered by the Minister; therefore no such prayer can be pretended. In the late Canon it is said, That the most reverent and humble gesture of the body in our meditation and lifting up of our hearts, best becommeth so divine an action. Meditation is not prayer, and the heart may be lifted up by the act of faith and

---

[1] *Sine statnibus non subsisteret mundus.*
[2] Page 95

contemplation, as well as by the action of prayer; so that neither public nor mental prayer is expressed in our act. But let the words be interpreted of mental prayer, even mental prayer is not the principal exercise of the soul in the act of receiving the sacramental elements: the mind attending on the audible words, the visible elements, the mystical actions, and making present use of them, men should not be diverted from their principal work and meditation, upon the Analogy betwixt the signs and things signified. The soul may send up in the mean time some short ejaculations and darts of prayer to heaven to strengthen her own weakness, and return to her principal work of meditation and application of the benefits represented. These short ejaculations of the mind are only occasional, as a Christian feeleth his own present estate, and are incident to all our actions both civil and religious: In the act of receiving our earthly food, in going out the way, in hearing the word. If a man be moved inwardly, when he heareth, that the word was made flesh, shall he kneel as they do in the Roman Kirk? If a man should kneel at every inward motion of the mind, when he heareth the word, what confusion would there be in the congregation? A man looking occasionally to a crucifix, may remember Christ, and send up some ejaculations, shall he therefore kneel? The three children prayed mentally no doubt when they were brought before the golden Image, but lawfully they might not kneel before it. Perkins distinguisheth notably betwixt public, private, and secret worship:[1] the secret and mental worship must be yielded to God, and the signs thereof concealed from the eyes and hearing of men, as Nehemiah when he prayed in presence of the King, *Nehemiah 2:4*. In a word, the Institution, and the second commandment hinder kneeling at this time, suppose mental prayer were the principal exercise of the soul. I hear there is alleged a third sort of prayer, to wit, that the very act of receiving is of itself a real prayer. Is not this as

---

[1] Idolatry page 700

much as to say, that craving and receiving is all one? Bellarmine[1] saith, That prayer of itself, and of the own proper office, doth impetrate, and that a sacrifice hath the force and power of obtaining, or impetrating: because it is, *Quaedam oratio realis, non verbalis*, a certain real prayer, not a verbal. We may forgive him to say this of the sacrifice of the Mass, where there is an offering of a sacrifice to God. But Bellarmine was never so absurd as to call the act of receiving from God, a real prayer to God.

Their other objection that we may praise God in the act of receiving; therefore we may kneel, may be answered after the same manner. There is no public thanksgiving ordained to be made at the delivery of the elements: mental praise therefore must be meant. Mental praise is no more the principal work of the soul, then mental prayer; what was said of the ejaculations of the one, let it be applied to the short ejaculations of the other. The name of Eucharist given to this Sacrament, helpeth them nothing: for it is a name given by Ancients, and not by the Scripture. Next, as it is called *Eucharistia*, so it is called[2] *Eulogia*: for the words, he gave thanks, and he blessed, are indifferently used by the Evangelists. Some parts of this holy celebration stand in thanksgiving, as the beginning and the end: and therefore is the whole action denominated from a part, saith[3] Causaubon. *Eulogia & Eucharistia utraque vox à parte una totum Domini actionem designat*. It followeth not that all the parts of this holy ministration are actions of thanksgiving.

Objection. What we may crave of God upon our knees, we may receive on our knees.

Answer. It is false, I may on my knees, Give us this day our daily bread; but I may not receive it on my knees. The people of Israel prayed for food, yet they were not esteemed unthankful, for not kneeling when they received the Manna.

---

[1] De Missa l. 2. c. 4
[2] Cyril. Epist. 10. con. Nestor. in council Ephesine
[3] Exercit. page 517

It is again objected, that in the act of receiving, we receive from Christ an inestimable benefit, ought not a subject kneel when he receiveth a benefit from a Prince to testify his thankfulness? Answer, this relation from Christ to the Sacrament, as between the giver and the gift is common to all the Sacraments both of the old, and new law, ordinary, and extraordinary. Next we receive the mystical pledges, not out of the hands of God himself or his Son Christ immediately, but out of the hand of the Minister. The person who receiveth the gift from the King, is supposed to receive it immediately: and suppose mediately, yet ceremonies of Court, & mediate civil worships, are not rules of religious adoration; which should ever be immediate. Thirdly the manner of delivery of the gift and the will of the giver, are to be considered. If the Prince call his Nobles to a banquet, it is his will that they sit at table with him, as Jonathan and David sat at King Saul's table. Christ has declared by the Institution, after what manner he would have us receive these mystical pledges. Kneeling cannot agree with the actions and precepts of the Institution.

The second breach of the second commandment made by kneeling, is, the shew of conformity with the papists. The Lord forbade his people to be like the Gentiles, *Leviticus 18:3* and *19:27* & *Deuteronomy 12*. The Christians were forbidden to décor[ate] their houses with bay leaves, and green boughs, because the pagans used so to do, or to rest from their labors, those days that the Pagans did. If conformity in things not having state in Idolatrous service, but only glancing at the honor of the Idol, be condemned; far more is conformity in the grossest act, wherein the life and soul as it were of their Idolatry standeth, Such as is the gesture of kneeling among the papists. And for this cause Hooper[1] in his sermon before King Edward, for the same cause condemned this gesture. This outward conformity tickleth the papist, and offendeth the godly.

---

[1] On Jonas [sermon?] 6

The third breach of the second commandment made by kneeling is, the retaining of a monument of vile idolatry. All human inventions polluted with idolatry, except they be of necessary use, ought to be removed from God's service. This gesture had a spot of profanation from the beginning, being at the first birth in this act dedicat[ed] to Idolatry. The brazen serpent set up at God's own command, was not spared when it was abused. We detest the very garment of a thief, or a whore, though it be innocent. Beza[1] saith, many things may be tolerate[d] for the weak, which may not be restored after they are tane [taken] away. He commendeth them, who have abolished kneeling amongst other things *tanquam apertas Idolomanias*.

The fourth breach of the 2nd commandment made by kneeling, is, the continual occasion and danger of idolatry. We are forbidden all occasions and provocations of idolatry. There is a natural proneness in all men to idolatry; great ignorance in the common people, and Superstition rooted in the hearts of men: Papists daily increase, the idol of the bready God is still in great accompt [account] in the Roman Kirks round about us, and in private corners amongst us: and yet men are not ashamed to say, that all memory of former superstition is past, and no peril is to be feared again. The virgins in Cyprian's time granted they walked with young men, talked with them, went to bed with them, but when it came to the act they abstained. Cyprian[2] answereth, *Nou est locus dandus diabolo: nemo diu tutus periculo proximus*. Place should not be given to the devil, no man is long safe who is near the point of danger. The Belgic Kirks in their Synods permitted not liberty of kneeling, for the same respect of bread-worship as may be seen in, the harmony of their Synods, set forth of late by Festus Homius[3], *Liberum est stando, sedendo, vel eundo caenam celebrare non autem geniculando ob*

---

[1] Epist. 8
[2] Lib. 1. ep. 11
[3] Cap. 13

artolatreias periculum. If a lawful use could be devised yet this danger cannot be eschewed. Information by preaching is a sufficient remedy: meat doth not nourish so fast as poison doeth corrupt. The watchmen are some time ignorant, or negligent, many want doctrine. It is better to fill up the pit, then to set one beside it to warn the passengers that they fall not in, such ceremonies ought to be appointed, which by their goodness and edification may help the preaching of the word, and not such as the word must daily have need to correct. The strength of many poor Christian souls should not be tried by bringing them to the very brink of danger.

The fifth breach of the second commandment made by kneeling, is, a shew of wisdom in will-worship and humility, *Colossians 2:23* a worship is set up by mans voluntary devotion in a principal part of God's service, under color of humility. We ought to come indeed, and receive with humility these mystical pledges: but is there no reverence and humility, but in kneeling? Swarez[1] saith that humility and adoration are distinguished, in their proper motives and respects, *in propriis honestatibus et motivis*. It was not mannerly for the disciples to use any gesture they pleased at Christ's table. It was his honor to command, and their humility to obey. Sitting was not pomp, glorious pride, or profane gesture, as men are not ashamed so to call it; because it was obedience to the Lord. This their pretended humility, is a natural humility; like unto Peter's, when he refused that Christ should wash his feet. Obedience is better then sacrifice. Fenner in the doctrine of the Sacraments[2] hath a notable saying, (that the whole honor of the Sacraments is, that they remain unto the Church of God in that simplicity he left them; and that no action here is worth any thing, but by reason of God's word, which is sanctified to a profitable use, and made an instrument of the working of the Holy Ghost.)

---

[1] *Tom. 1. Disp. 51. sect. 1*
[2] Pag. 130

Objection. There is no new worship appointed, but an action already appointed for God's service is applied to the said Supper. *Answer.* The parts of God's worship may not be applied to other when comeliness, commodiousness, institution, and command will not suffer. A man may not kneel all the time of the Sermon; he may not read in the act of receiving; baptism may not be ministered in the midst of the communion, and many such instances might be alleged. Aquinas saith,[1] *Superstuum in his quae ad divinum cultum pertinent esse potest no secundum substantiam quanti, sed secundum alias circumstantias, puta quia cultus divinus exhibetur cui non debet exhiberi vel quado non debet vel secudum alias circumstantias prout non debet.* That superfluity in things pertaining to the worship of God, is to be considered, not according to the quantity, for we cannot worship God exceedingly enough: but is to be considered according to other circumstances, viz. when the worship of God is not exhibited to whom it ought to be exhibited, or when it ought not, according to other circumstances, as it ought not to be exhibited. By superfluity he meaneth excess, a vice in all moral virtues. To be short, a rite Sacramental, devised by man, pretending humility, and shouldering out other rites instituted by God, cannot be but presumptuous will-worship. Such is the gesture of kneeling, as we have already proved.

Obiection. The Eucharist is a part of God's worship, therefore we ought to kneel in the act of receiving.

Answer. In a large sense every act whereby God is honored may be called the worship of God, as oaths, vows, sacrifices, &c. But adoration is the worship of God in a strict sense. Kneeling is the gesture of adoration, but not of every part of God's worship. Receiving, eating, drinking in the sacrament, are parts of God's worship, but they are not gestures of adoration. All the Sacraments both of Jews and Christians, were parts of God's worship as well as the Eucharist, and yet they kneeled not in the act of participation.

---

[1] 2.2. *quest.* 81. *ad* 5

Objection. The Eucharist is a sacrifice, and *congeries sacrificiorum*, a heap of sacrifices, a commemorative sacrifice, a sacrifice of a broken and contrite hart, of praise, of prayer, of alms, therefore this Sacrament should be received with kneeling, saith the B. of Rochester[1]: and therefore the gesture of kneeling is rightly applied to such a kind of worship.

Answer. The actions aforesaid are called sacrifices, only by analogy and metaphorically, they are not proper sacrifices: the invisible Sacrifice by the which a man offereth himself by contrition, inward devotion, mortification is the daily Sacrifice of a Christian, *Romans 13:1* we offer ourselves to be sacrificed when the word is preached, *Romans 15* we kneel not when we give alms. These improper and metaphorical sacrifices, are not acts of adoration.[2] The paschal lamb was slain in the manner of a real sacrifice, and yet notwithstanding of this immolation, they kneeled not at the eating of the paschal lamb. The Sacraments of the Old and New Testament were alike in representation, signification, and exhibition. Of prayer and praise we spake before in particular.

Kneeling not practiced in the ancient Kirk.

The former two breaches are sufficient of themselves, howbeit kneeling were otherwise warranted by the practice of the Kirk: but as it had no warrant from Scripture, & reason, so likewise it wanteth the warrant of antiquity. When the Arians denied Christ's true divinity, the orthodox Kirk acknowledging his divinity, kneeled not in the act of receiving which was expedient if it had been lawful: because the Arians debased the Son of God. It was the custom of the Kirk to stand in time of public prayer upon all the Lord's Days in the year, and every day from Easter to Pentecost, as witnesseth Tertullian, Cyprian, Basilius, Jerome, Augustine, Hugo de

---

[1] Discours. p. 84

[2] *Swarez. tom. 1. disput. 51. sect, 2. Est autem ridiculum dicere Elecmosynam esse actu adorationis.*

sancto Victore, Anselmus, the Council of Nice, the 6th Council of Carthage, The Council of Constantinople, Quinisextum, the Council of Turone. The testimonies are set down in the B. of Rochester his discourse. Bellarmine closeth all up in one general, to wit, that in his time five hundreth years were not past, since the rite to pray standing & not kneeling on the Lord's Day had ceased.[1] If they kneeled not in the time of prayer where this gesture is most requisite by their own confession, because of the joyful memory of Christ's resurrection, far less did they kneel in the act of banqueting and receiving the inestimable gifts offered unto us in this sacrament, a matter of great joy. Wherefore served the signification of standing in prayer, if it was controlled with the gesture of an humble penitentiary at the sacrament? The testimony alleged by the B. of Rochester[2] out of Tertullian, that they that were to be baptized, must pray with often prayers, and fastings, and kneelings, and watchings, proveth neither kneeling on the Lord's Day in time of prayer, or the act of baptism, but only declareth what were the exercises of preparation on the days preceding baptism. In the assembly holden last at St. Andrews, standing or kneeling in time of public prayer was left to every mans liberty. In the Assembly holden at Perth, they have tane [taken] away this liberty in the act of receiving. They left liberty in the act of public humiliation, and have tane [taken] it away in the act of mental meditation. Let any man therefore judge of their intention. The authors above rehearsed make not all mention of prayer, when they speak of standing: but generally they speak against kneeling on the Lord's Day. Tertullian[3] saith generally *de geniculis adorare*, to adore upon the knees upon the Lord's Day is unlawful. He saith not *orare*, but *adorare*. Hierom[4] his testimony also is general against adoration on the knees. Pope

---

[1] *De cultis sanctor. c. 11*
[2] Pag. 177
[3] *De Coron. milit.*
[4] *Contra Luciferanos*

Alexander the 3rd hath their words. *Quonia diebus aute dominicis & alijs praecipuis sestivitatibus suis inter pascha & Pentecosten genuum flexio nequaquam debet fieri:*[1] *nisi aliquis ex deuotione id velit facere in secreto. In consecrationibus aute Episcoporum & Clericoru ordinationibus consecrans & consecratus tantum genua flectere possunt secundum quod consecrationis modus requrit.* Upon the Lord's Day and other chief festivities, and between Easter and Pentecost there ought to be no kneeling, except one will do it in secret of devotion. In the consecration of Bishops and ordination of clergy-men he that consecrateth and he that is consecrated, may only bow their knees, so far as the form of consecration requireth. If this was the only exception, it followeth that in no other case, they did kneel on these days. *Exceptio firmat regulam in casibus non exceptis.* They received the communion usually upon the Lord's Day: and therefore it was called the day of bread[2]. Yea and in some places only upon the Lord's Day, as Jewel observeth[3] out of an Epistle sent from the council of Alexandria in the defense of one Macarius. Tertullian expressly affirmeth, that the manner was to stand at the receiving[4]. Dionysius Alexandrinus writeth to Xistus concerning one who standing at the table had often received the holy food in these words. *Nonne solennior erit statio tua si ad aram Dei steteris accepto corpore Domini.*[5] Chrysostom[6] saith, *Stemus trementes & timidi demissis oculis renata autem anima gementes siue jubilantes corde.* Let us stand trembling, &c. The Alyssines receive the sacrament standing even to this day, as also the Muscouites, howbeit drowned otherwise in great superstition, receive the Sacrament standing.

---

[1] *Decretal. lib. 2. tit. 9. de ferijs cap.*
[2] *Chrysost. hom. 5. de resurrectione*
[3] *Artic. 1. Divis. 25*
[4] *De orat.*
[5] *Euseb. lib. 7. cap. 8*
[6] *Homil. in Encenijs*

Ojection. The Ethincks [pagans] objected to Christians that they did honor Bacchus and Ceres; and Averroes, that they adored that which they did eat. Theodoret saith[1] the mystical signs are adored. Augustine[2] no man eateth that flesh before he adore it. Ambrose[3] we adore the flesh of Christ in the mysteries Chrysostom saith,[4] let us imitate the Barbarians, thou beholdst him not in a manger, but on an Altar. And again,[5] they are like Herod, who adore not the Eucharist.

Answer. It followeth not they adored, therefore they kneeled. The Ethnicks did mistake the reverend and grave behavior of Christians at the receiving the Sacrament, as they did many other things both in Jews and Christians: they gave out that they were worshippers of the clouds, of the Son of the cross, of the head of an Ass, of the slaughter of infants. Augustine saith. *A Cerere & Libero paganorum dijs longè absumus quamvis panis & calicis sacramentum nostro ritu amplectimur*.[6] We are far from Ceres & Bacchus the gods of the Pagans, howbeit we embrace the Sacrament of the bread & the cup after our rite. When Theodoret saith the mystical signs are adored,[7] he meaneth by adoration, reverend and religious handling, as becometh so great mysteries: and so Bilson: exponeth [expounds] Theodoret, and to this purpose allegeth the glosse [interpretation] of the Canon Law,[8] *In hoc sensu possumus quamlibet rem sacram adorare, id est reverentiam exhibere*. Anastasius saith,[9] *Dominica verba attentè audiant, & fideliter adorent*. Let them diligently hear, & faithfully adore the word of God. The word adoration is sometime taken in a large sense for veneration; so do all our Divines expone

---

[1] *Dialog.* 2
[2] *In psalm* 98
[3] *Lib.* 3. *cap.* 12. *de spirit. sanct.*
[4] *Homil.* 24 *in* 1 *Corinthians*
[5] *Homil.* 7. *in Mattheum*
[6] *Contra Faustum*
[7] *Obedience p.* 534,557
[8] *De consecrat. dist.* 3. *venerabilis*
[9] *De consecrat. dist.* 1. *Apostolica*

[expound] Theodoret, or else his phrase were absurd: and indeed none of the Fathers used that phrase but he. Chrysostom's Homilies on Matthew are a supposititious work. The rest of the testimonies alleged make mention of adoration, not of the Sacrament, but of Christ in the Sacrament: and they are to be understood of spiritual and internal adoration, common to this sacrament with other sacraments. Augustine saith, The flesh of Christ is adored either in the sacrifice, or otherwise by faith[1]. The adoration is as the eating, the eating is spiritual and by faith. Augustine speaking of the veneration of this sacrament, saith,[2] *Contemptum solum non vult cibus ille.* That meat misliketh only contempt, as Manna did loathsomeness. Ambrose speaketh of all the mysteries of Christian[3] Religion. Chrysostom is to be understood of spiritual reverence[4]: and therefore he useth emphatical speeches of ascending up to the gates of heaven, even of the heaven of heavens, like Eagles. For the same Chrysostom saith,[5] that we adore Christ in Baptism. None of all the testimonies alleged expresseth any gesture of the body, let be kneeling.

Objection. For an humble gesture are alleged Origen[6]: Thou therefore humbling thyself, imitate the Centurion, and say, Lord I am not worthy, &c. Cyrillus of Jerusalem[7], Then after the communion of the body of Christ, come also to the cup of his blood, not reaching out thy hands, but falling on thy face in manner of adoration and worship, say Amen. Nazianzen[8] saith, his sister fell down before the Altar, and called on him who was worshipped on the Altar.

---

[1] *Fulk. 1 Cor. 11. sect. 18*
[2] *Epist. 118*
[3] *Fulk. 1 Cor. 11. sect. 18*
[4] *Fulk ibid.*
[5] *Hom. 14. in Marcum*
[6] *Homil. 15 in divers. locos.*
[7] *In cateches. mystugogic*
[8] *In Epitaph. Gorgonia*

Answer. Origen directs the words to be said as well when the preacher entereth into our house, as when we receive the sacrament.[1] Further, Possevinus a learned Papist, acknowledgeth that work to be counterfeit.[2] The Catechisms attributed to Cyril of Jerusalem is a book newly sprung up, and unknown to the Ancients. It was not to be found in Harding's time, but in writing. See Moulin's translated[3]. This counterfeit Cyril saith not, *Cade pronus*, fall down on thy face; but, *accede pronus*, come inclining, or bowing thy body; as men use to do when they make courtesy. Nazianzen's sister was sick in body, and sick in mind: her fact was private, and in the dark of the night, she was not in the act of receiving the sacrament, she blubbered with her tears the fragments of the sacrament received before. Christ is honored at the Altar, or communion-table, by the administration of the sacrament celebrated to his honor and worship, in remembrance of him: his mercies are there laid forth in the mysteries. Ye see no testimony can be alleged for geniculation. The Council of Constantinople holden under the Emperor Basilius, hath these words: *Jesus Christus panis substantiam mandavit apponi, ne scilicet humana effigie figurata idolatria introduceretur.* For eschewing of Idolatry, the Lord commanded the substance of bread to be set on without any human shape. The proofs already made for standing upon the Lord's Day, for 1000 years in the Kirk, do evince that geniculation had no place in the act of receiving all that time. It was therefore followed upon bodily presence and transubstantiation.

Kneeling not practiced in the Reformed Churches.

The Lutheran Kirks do acknowledge real presence by way of consubstantiation: it is no wonder therefore that they approve kneeling. The reformed Kirks as they have damned

---

[1] *Bilson, Obedience. p.* 540
[2] *Riveti specimen critici sacri. lib.* 2. *cap* 13
[3] *Part* 2. *pag* 65

bodily presence, so have they rejected this gesture of kneeling in the act of receiving. The Kirk of Bohemia hath retained this gesture since the days of John Hus. In their confession exhibited to King Ferdinand, *Anno* 1535 it is thus said,[1] *Ministeri verò Dominicae caenae verba referentes plebem ipsam ad hanc fidem hortantur, ut corporis Christi presentiam adesse credant.* The Ministers are willed to stir up the people to believe that the body of Christ is present: the poorer sort amongst them, as they have rejected the error of real presence, so depart they from this gesture. In our neighbor Kirk some of their defenders of kneeling will not have us inquisitive of the manner of Christ's presence in the sacrament.[2] And the Bishop of Rochester commendeth the simplicity of the Ancients, which disputed not whether Christ was present Con, sub, in, or trans, in this Supper.[3] Sutton in his Appendix to his *Meditations on the Lord's Supper*, condemneth likewise this diligent search of the manner of Christ's presence. If the manner of Christ's presence be not determined, there can arise no other but a confused worship of such a confused and determinate presence. The Papists acknowledge that there ought to be no adoration but where there is acknowledged a bodily presence in the sacrament. Hence it is that they prove mutually the one by the other.

It will not follow that we may change sitting into kneeling, because the ancient Kirk and some reformed Kirks have changed sitting into standing; because kneeling maketh so many breaches both in the institution, and in the second commandment, and is no ways a table gesture. By standing we accommodate ourselves to a table to participate of the dainties set thereon, standing was never abused to idolatry as kneeling hath been. We are not bound to imitate other kirks further then they imitate Christ. Our sitting is not Scottish

---

[1] *Cap.* 15
[2] Hooker Eccles. polic. lib. 5. sect. 67
[3] *Discours. pag.* 35

Genevating, but a commendable imitation of the Apostolical Churches, and obedience to Christ's institution.

They flee up at last to the Kirk triumphant; and allege for kneeling the 24 Elders falling down before the Lamb, but how conclude they this, that they that are called to the Supper of the lamb kneel at the Supper of the lamb? And seeing the blessed souls shall not be clothed with their bodies before the resurrection, how can they conclude, material geniculation of the blessed Saints in heaven? All creatures in heaven, in earth, and under the earth; are said to bow their knee at the name of Jesus, that is, to acknowledge his sovereign authority, howbeit the celestial Angels, blessed souls, and infernal spirits, have not knees to bow with. The everlasting felicity of the children of God, is the Supper of glory. Do they drink continually of that felicity upon their knees? Thousand thousands stand before him, many shall come from the East, and from the West, and sit at the heavenly table with Abraham, Isaac, and Jacob: may we not then conclude sitting and standing, as well as they do kneeling, if we look to the letter of parables, visions, allegories and prophesies? But Symbolical Theology is not argumentative. Last, how will they prove evidently that the falling of the 24 Elders before the lamb, is to be interpreted of the Kirk triumphant, rather then of the Kirk Militant?

REASONS AGAINST FESTIVAL DAYS

From the beginning of the Reformation to this present year of our Lord 1618, the Kirk of Scotland hath diverse ways condemned the observation of all holy days, the Lord's Day only excepted. In the first chapter of the first book of discipline penned *Anno* 1560 the observation of holy days to Saints, the feast of Christmass, Circumcision, Epiphany, Purification, and other fond feasts of our Lady are ranked amongst the abominations of the Roman religion, as having neither commandment nor assurance in the word. It is farther affirmed that the obstinate maintainers & teachers of such abomination should not escape the punishment of the civil Magistrate. The book aforesaid was subscribed by the Lords of secret Council. In the general Assembly holden at Edinburgh *Anno* 1566, the latter confession of Helvetia was approved; but with special exception against some holy days dedicated to Christ; these same very days, that now are urged. In the Assembly holden *Anno* 1575 complaint was made against the Ministers and Readers beside Aberdeen, because they assembled the people to prayer and preaching upon certain patron and festival days. Complaint likewise was ordained to be made to the Regent upon the Town of Drumfries for urging, and convoying a Reader to the Kirk with Tabret and Whistle to read the prayers all the holy Days of Yule, or Christmas upon the refusal of their own Reader, Item an article was formed to be presented to the Regent, craving that all days heretofore keeped holy in time of Papistry beside the Lord's Day such as Yule day, Saints days, and other like feasts may be abolished, a civil penalty appointed against the observers of the said days. Banqueting, playing, feasting, and such other vanities upon the days foresaid is condemned. In the Assembly holden in April *Anno* 1577 it was ordained that the Visitor with the advice of the Synodal Assembly, shall admonish Ministers preaching or ministering the communion at[1] Pasche, Yule, or other like superstitious times or Readers reading, to desist, under the pain of deprivation. Dedicating of days was abjured in the confession of faith penned anno 1580. An Article was formed in the Assembly *Anno* 1581 craving an act of Parliament to be made against observation of feast days, dedicated to Saints, and setting out of bone-fires. In the Assembly holden in February *Anno* 1587 it was humbly moved to his Majesty, that Pasche and Yule was superstitiously observed in Fyffe, and about Drumfries. In the Assembly holden *Anno* 1590 his Majesty in open audience of the Assembly praised God for that he was borne to be a King in the sincerest Kirk in the world: sincerer then our neighbor Kirk of England: for their service was an evil-said Mass in English: Sincerer then Geneva itself: for they observed Pasche and Yule. In the Parliament holden *Anno* 1592 the act of King James the third anent the Saturday and other vigils to be kept holy from Even-song to Evensong was annulled. Item, the act made by Queen Regent granting license to keep Yule and Pasche. In the Assembly holden *Anno* 1596 when the covenant was renewed, superstition and Idolatry breaking forth in keeping of festival days, setting out of bone-fires, and singing of Carols, is reckoned amongst the corruptions which were to be amended. The Pulpits have sounded continually against all festival days. The Censures of the Kirk have been put in execution in all due form against the observers. In the pretended Assembly holden at Perth in August last past, it was concluded, that hereafter every Minister shall make commemoration of the inestimable benefits received from God, by and through our Lord and Saviour Jesus Christ, his

---

[1] *Easter and Christmas*

Birth, Passion, Resurrection, Ascension, and sending down of the Holy Ghost upon the days appointed for that use. That they shall make choice of several and pertinent Texts, and frame their Doctrine and exhortation accordingly. This their conclusion was ratified and allowed by act of Council, and proclamation was made thereupon, commanding cessation and abstinence from all kind of labor and handy-work upon the five days above written, that everyone may the better attend the holy exercises which are to be kept in the Kirk at these times. But first we will premit [state] the proper description of a festival day.

The description of a festival day

Piscator describeth a Festival day in this manner,[1] *Festum proprii loquendo est publica & solennis ceremonia mandata à Deo, ut certo anni tempore cum singulari loetitia obeatur ad gratias agendum Deo pro certo aliquo beneficio in populum suum collato.* A feast in proper speech is a public and solemn ceremony commanded by God to be celebrated a certain time of the year, with singular gladness to give thanks to God for some certain benefit bestowed on his people. Hooker entreating this argument intituleth [entitles] the subject festival days. He maketh festival solemnity to be nothing else, but the due mixture, as it were, of these three elements; Praises set forth with cheerful alacrity of mind: delight expressed by charitable largeness more then common bounty: and sequestration from ordinary labors.[2] By these descriptions we may see that the Sabbath day is not properly a festival day. The ordinary Sabbath is weekly: the festival is anniversary. We may fast upon the ordinary Sabbath, but we cannot fast and mourn upon a festival day, *Nehemiah 8:10* for that were to confound fasting and festival days. The Council of Laodicea inhibited to

---

[1] *Galat.* 4:9,10,11
[2] *Policy. lib. 5. sect. 7*

celebrate the feasts of martyrs in Lent, for the same regard upon the ordinary Sabbath all the parts of God's worship may be performed as occasion shall offer. Upon the festival days we are bound to the commemoration of a particular benefit. Proper texts, Epistles, Gospels, Homilies, and sermons are framed for the mystery of that day. So that the ordinary Sabbath is moral and for the worship of God in general, the festival is mystical. *Esentialia festi*, the essential parts of a festival day are cessation from work: hearing of the word: participation of the sacraments. Commemoration of divine mysteries may be performed upon the ordinary Sabbath, but to make up a festival day Bellarmine[1] requireth a determination of a day, signification and representation of the mysteries wrought on such days. Scaliger[2] observeth that the ordinary Sabbaths were never called *Chaggim* as the anniversary solemnities were.

1. Reason against festival days

Six days shalt thou labor and do all that thou hast to do. These words are either a command to do the works of our calling as many both Jewish and Christian divines do interpret: or else a permission, as others do interpret. If they contain a command, no countermand may take it away. If a permission, no human authority may spoil men of the liberty that God hath granted unto them, as long as they have any manner of work to do for the sustentation of this life. The Muscovites therefore say very well: that it is for Lords to keep feasts, and abstain from labor. The Citizens and Artificers amongst them upon the festival days after divine service, do betake themselves to their labor, and domestic affairs, as Gaguinus reporteth,[3] It may be objected that Constantine the Emperor made a law that none but the Prince may *ferias co*

---

[1] *De cultu sanctorum. lib. 3. cap.* 10
[2] *Addenda prolegomenia in lib. de emendat. temp.*
[3] *Cod. lib. 3. Art.* 12. l. 4

dere, erect an idle day: the Prince then may enjoin a day of Cessation. *Answer*. The Laws of the Code are not rules of theology. A Prince may not enjoin Cessation from Economical and domestic works but for weapon shewing, exercise of arms, defense of the country or other public works and affaires. But that is not to enjoin a day of simple Cessation, but to enjoin a politick work in place of the economical. Every particular member ceasing from their particular work exerciseth another work serving for the preservation of the whole body. The curse that Adam shall eat with the sweat of his brows, is mitigated by the permission of six days labor. The Lord permitteth unto man six, lest he devour the seventh day which is sanctified. What if the Kirk representative enjoin a weekly holy day, as another Sabbath, ought the Kirk to be obeyed? What power hath the Kirk representative, to enjoin an anniversary day more then a weekly or hebdomadary [weekly] holy day. If a day of simple Cessation from all manner of work Economical and political may not be enjoined, a festival day may not be enjoined. I say further that the poor craftsman cannot lawfully be commanded to lay aside his tools, and go pass his time, no not for an hour, let be for a day as long as he is willing to work, and perhaps urged with the sharpness of present necessity. And yet farther that he ought not to be compelled to leave his work to go to divine service except on the day that the Lord hath sanctified.

The second Reason.

It is the privilege of God's power to appoint a day of rest, and to sanctify it to his honor, as our best Divines[1] maintain. Zanchius[2] affirmeth that it is proper to God to choose any person or any thing to consecrate and sanctify it to himself, as it belongeth to him alone to justify, *Catechismus Hollandicus*

---

[1] *Perkins, Gal. 4. Willets Synops. pag. 501 & Rom. 14 controvers. 4 Kuchlinus in Catechis. Holland. de diebus festis.*
[2] *In 4. praecept. col. 655*

saith no wise man will deny that this sanctification belongeth only to God, & that it is manifest sacrilege to attribute these things to men, which are only of divine ordination. Willet saith: It belongeth only to the Creator to sanctify the Creature. In the book of *Ecclesiasticus*, cap. 33:7,8 it is demanded, Why doth one day excel another, when as the light of every day of the year is of the Sun? It is answered, By the knowledge of the Lord they were distinguished, and he altered seasons and feasts. Some of them hath he made high days, and hallowed them; Some of them he hath made ordinary days. The common tenet of the Divines was acknowledged by the pretended Bishop of Galloway in his Sermon at the last Christmas. It may offend you, said he, that this is an holy day. I say there is no power either civil or Ecclesiastical can make an holy day: no King, no Kirk: only the Lord that made the day, and distinguished it from the night: he hath sanctified the seventh day. The like was acknowledged by M. P. Galloway in his Christmas Sermons. If the special sanctification of a day to an holy use dependeth upon God's commandment and institution, then neither King nor Kirk representative may make an holy day.

The observers of days will say they count not their anniversary days holier then other days, but that they keep them only for order and policy, that the people may be assembled to religious exercises. *Answer*. The Papists will confess that one day is not holier then another in its own nature, no not the Lord's Day: for then the Sabbath might not have been changed from the last, to the first day of the week. But they affirm that one day is holier then another, in respect of the end and use; And so do we. They call them holy days: and so do we. They use them as memorial signs of sacred mysteries whereof they carry the names, as Nativity; Passion; Ascension. &c. And so do we. The presence of the festivity putteth a man in mind of the mystery, howbeit he have not occasion to be present in the holy Assembly. We are commanded to observe them in all points as the Lord's Day, both in the public Assemblies, and after the dissolving of the same. Yea it is left free to teach any part of God's word on the Lord's Day; but for solemnity of the festival, solemn texts must be chosen: Gospels Epistles, collects, Psalms must be framed for the particular service of these days, and so the mystical days of mans appointment, shall not only equal, but in solemnity surpass the moral Sabbath appointed by the Lord. Doth not Hooker say that the days of public memorials should be clothed with the outward robes of holiness, They allege for the warrant of anniversary festivities the Ancients, who call them Sacred and mystical days. If they were instituted only for order and policy, that the people may assemble to religious exercises, wherefore is there but one day appointed betwixt the Passion and Resurrection? Forty days betwixt the Resurrection and Ascension? Ten betwixt the Ascension and Pentecost? Wherefore follow we the course of the Moon as the Jews did, in our moveable feasts making the Christian Church clothed with the Sun to walk under the Moon, as[1] Bonaventura alludeth? Wherefore is there not a certain day of the month kept for Easter, as well as for the nativity? Doth not Bellarmine give this reason out of Augustine that the day of the Nativity is celebrate[d] only for memory, the other both for memory; and for sacraments.[2] *Ille celebratur solum ob memoriam, & ideo semper die 25. Decembris: at isfe celebratur ob memoriam & sacramentum, & ideo variatur*. If the anniversary commemorations were like the weekly preachings, as the two forenamed preachers made the comparison, why is the husbandman forced to leave his plough at the one, and not at the other? Why hath the one proper service and not the other? Why did not M. Galloway curse the people for absence from the one, as well as from the other? Why are the days of the one changeable, and not the other? To make solemn commemoration of Christ's nativity upon any other day, then upon the putative [supposed] day of

---

[1] *Lib. 2. Dist. 4. unmer. 48*
[2] *De cultu sanct. Lib. 3. Cap. 12*

his nativity, would be thought a great absurdity; siclike [such like] of his Passion, Ascension. &c. And last, how could M. Galloway affirm that the evidence of God's Spirit appeared in the Christmas Sermons that are extant, more lively then in any other Sermons?

Next it may be objected that the people of God might have indicted days of fasting at their own determination, and an interdiction of all kind of work. Answer. They had a general warrant from God, *Joel 2:15* to proclaim a general fast, according to the occurrence of their calamities and other affaires of the Kirk. The light and law of nature leadeth a man to this observation of an occasional fast: nature teacheth him presently to withdraw his hand and heart from worldly affaires, and to lift them up to God to deprecate his wrath when his judgment is above our heads. The like may be said, by analogy, of thanksgiving, that we ought to praise God in the mean time when we receive the benefit. But to make of the occasional days of fasting, or feasting, anniversary and set festival and fasting days is without warrant. It remaineth therefore that it is the Lord's sovereignty to make or ordain a thing to be holy. God first sanctifies by commandment and institution: man sanctifieth thereafter by observation, applying to an holy use the time sanctified by God. It was a part of the Idolatry of the golden calf to proclaim a holy day. It is numbered among one of Jeroboam's sins that he ordained a feast after the devise of his own heart, *1 Kings 12:33*. Musculus[1] saith, If any man shall attempt to make holy at his pleasure the things that God hath not Sanctified, is not only Superstitious, but challengeth unto himself, that which belongs only to God. When God blesseth and sanctifieth a day, then may man look for a blessing in sanctifying it.

---

[1] *Loci. communes praec.* 4

The third Reason.

We come from privilege to fact. As *de jure* none may, so *de facto* none did, appoint holy days under the law but God, and that either by himself, or by some extraordinary direction. Therefore none can be allowed under the Gospel without the like warrant. Seeing the times under the Gospel are not so ceremonious, as the times under the law. Against this reason two instances are commonly alleged the one of the days of Purim instituted by Mordecai: the other of the feast of dedication instituted by Judas Maccabeus, and graced with Christ's presence, as is alleged, *John 10*. But the answer is easy.

The days of Purim were simply called the days of Purim: not the holy days of Purim. They are neither called *Chag*, nor *Mogned*, nor *Gnatsarah* as the other anniversary feasts are called in the Old Testament. No mention is made of holy convocations on these days nor divine service proper to them, notwithstanding of their return to the temple, and promise that the memorial of the days of Purim should not fall from among them, nor perish from their seed, *Esther 9:27,28*. It is true that now a days they read the book of Esther. And therefore call it the feast of Megilla, after the reading whereof they spend the rest of the time in reveling, more mad than the Gentiles were in their Bacchanalis. This reading was not the first institution, but an addition of the later Jews, The days of Purim were instituted only for civil days, and the ordinance required no farther, but that they should make them days of feasting and joy, and sending of portions one to another, and gifts to the poor, *Esther 9:19,22* to be documents and testimonies of their fasting and crying, that is in remembrance of their fasting and prayers, by which they obtained that deliverance. At the instant time of their delivery, it is said they rested, but in the Edict when the days were made anniversary, rest from all kind of work was not forbidden:

therefore Hospinian[1] saith, *In festo Phurim operari prohibitum non est*: they were not forbidden to work. And Willet compareth it with the fifth of November,[2] and affirmeth the like. Next, it is to be considered, that Mordecai is thought to be the pen-man of the book of Esther, and consequently a Prophet. He was one of the 120 masters of the great Synagogue, amongst whom were both Priests and Prophets, Ezra, and his society, Daniel & his companions, Zachary, Malachy, &c. Thirdly, it appeareth, *Esther 9:28* that it was an order to endure, as long as the feast days appointed by the Lord himself, and in no case to be altered. Holy days of Ecclesiastical constitution are not of such a nature, as[3] D. Fulk acknowledgeth. Whatsoever therefore was the quality of these days, whether holy or civil, the warrant was more then ordinary.

The Feast of Dedication, whereof mention is made, *John 10* some take for the dedication of the Temple in Zerubbabel's time, as the[4] Magdeburg Centuries. So likewise Chrysostom, Theophilactus, Cajetanus, Abulensis, Euthymius, and others, as[5] Barradius reporteth. But let it be meant, as is alleged: If the feast of dedication in Solomon and Zerubbabel's time was anniversary, then the Maccabees did follow the example of these who had Prophetical direction. If they were not anniversary, as indeed[6] Toletus leaveth it as uncertain, then this annual memory was an addition of the Pharisees, who enlarged the glory of this feast, as they did their Phylacteries. Junius[7] relateth out of the Talmud, that the wise men decreed that the eight days of that feast should be yearly days of joy. By the wise men are meant the Pharisees, who were called

---

[1] *De origine festorum Judaeorum*
[2] *Synopsis controversie of holydayes*
[3] *Against the Rhemists Apoc. 1:10*
[4] *Cent. 1. Col. 244*
[5] *Comment in Evangel. Tom 3. lib. 4. cap. 16*
[6] *In John* 10
[7] *John* 10

Sapientes Israelis. The renewment of the Altar, and of certain other decayed places, was honored by them with an annual memory, whereas the whole Temple, with all the implements and furniture thereof in Solomon and Zerubbabel's time had not the like honor. Neither do we read that any annual memory was instituted by Hezekiah after the profanation of the Temple by Ahaz and Urijah: nor by Josiah, after that it was polluted by Manasseh & Amon. Christ's walking in Solomon's Porch, maketh nothing for approbation of this feast. He had remained in Jerusalem from the feast of the Tabernacles, and came not up of purpose to keep that feast. He taketh old of the present opportunity to thrust his sickle into a thick harvest.

We have to consider for a general answer to all instances alleged from the Jewish Kirk, first that they had extraordinary directions which we want. They had prophets by office, or commission, who ended in Malachi. They had prophets who were only prophets by the Spirit as Daniel, David, and Solomon, who endured after the days of Malachi, as Drusius[1] affirmeth They had Urim and Thummim under the first Temple, and in place thereof, a slender voice sounding from the heaven, called *Bathkol*, under the second Temple, as Tremellius[2] hath observed. Next the Pharisees and degenerating Jews filled their Calendar with fond feasts of their own invention, as the festivities of the Equinoctial and festival days, other ways called the feasts of the *Tekuphas*: or converted any ancient order into a solemn feast, as the day appointed for carrying wood to the Temple to maintain the fire of the altar, *Nehemiah 10:34* they turned into a feast called the feast of *Xylophoria*. A holy day is to be observed not by a few but by all: but all were not appointed to bring wood, but those only who were designed by lot. It is no wonder therefore that they took the like course with the days of Purim. But we are not to imitate the Pharisees, and fond Jews.

---

[1] *In 2 Peter 1:21*
[2] *In Acts 12:22*

The fourth Reason.

The observation of anniversary days pertained to the ceremonial law: but so it is that the ceremonial law is abolished. The anniversary days were distinguished from the moral Sabbath. Many were the preeminences of the ordinary Sabbath above the anniversary. 1. It was more ancient, given to Adam in the state of innocence. 2. Uttered by God's own mouth. 3. Written with God's own finger in durable stone. 4. The Lord himself in a manner rested on it, when as he rained not Manna that day. 5. It was more strictly observed, then the other holy days, therefore some say it was called *Shabbath, Shabbathon*. Therefore likewise [likewise] the Jews measured unto it a Sabbath day's journey. 6. Other holy days were celebrated either in remembrance of a by-past benefit, or to signify something to come. It excelled them in both, faith[1] Bellarmine. 7. Other holy days gave place unto it The Jews made a Canon, that two Sabbaths should not concur together *propter olera & propter mortuos,* that is, because they could not keep in that hot region their sodden meats two days together; nor the bodies of the dead unburied for stink, and putrefaction. Therefore they transferred this Sabbath of extraordinary solemnity immediately proceeding the ordinary Sabbath to the ordinary Sabbath. They were drawn to it, it was never drawn to them, See[2] Causabonus. In a word, the Jews held it in greater estimation, then the rest. They called it the Queen of the holy days, and the secret of the living God. The three solemnities called *Regalim* were Temple feasts. They were bound to celebrate them at the Temple the public theater of all the Jewish ceremonies The Apostle calleth them weak and beggarly elements, *Galatians 4:9,10* the elements of the world, *Colossians 2:20* shadows of things to come, *Colossians*

---

[1] *De cultu sanctorum, lib.* 3. *cap.* 11
[2] *De exercitat. p.* 482

2:16,17. The Apostle saith not the observation of Judaical days, but simpliciter [simply], the observation of days served to the people of God for a typical use, and a rudiment of religion. If the observation of some anniversary days was prescribed to the Jews, as elements and rudiments for their instruction; it followeth that the observation of anniversary days is of itself a rudimentary instruction; otherwayes [otherwise] the Apostle's reason will not hold. The Apostle condemneth difference of days as he condemneth difference of meats. To esteem some meats clean, and some unclean is Judaical, howbeit we observe not the same difference, that the Jews did. Days and meats are paralleled together, to esteem one day holier then another, not so discerned by the Lord's commandment must be also Judaical. The Kirk under the Gospel hath past the rudiments; and therefore the observation of anniversary days doth not beseem her. To substitute other days in place of the Jewish, a Christian Pasche and Pentecost for the Jewish, is but to substitute rudiments and elements to the Jewish, & not to chase away, but to change the Jewish holy days, as Bellarmine doth[1] *Non est sublata sed mutata significatio et discretio dierum.* The Jewish frankincense was a perfume: the Popish is a simple frankincense without any other ingredient. The Jewish lights were of oil: the popish of wax and yet we charge them with Judaizing. The Jews had no anniversary days, but such as were abrogate, they were abrogate not only as shadows of things to come, but also as memorials of bygone benefits. Even as they were days of remembrance they belonged to the pedagogy of the law. Converted Jews may not lawfully observe the Jewish festivities, even as remembrances of bygone benefits. In every respect all their anniversary days are abolished, and they had none other, but such as were abolished. Therefore in every respect they belonged to the ceremonial Law. The observation therefore of anniversary days even in respect of remembrance was to the Jews

---

[1] *De cultu Sanctorum c.* 10

pedagogical, rudimentary and elementary, and consequently ceremonial. The Bishop of Chester[1] confesseth that all the solemn feasts were of a ceremonial nature. If the Jews had no anniversary solemnities to endure after Christ's coming when they should be converted to Christianism, how can the observation of anniversary days be taken up by Christians?

The fifth Reason.

The prerogative belonging to God in the Old Testament, was transferred to Christ, God and Man, the law-giver in the New Testament, one that was faithful in all the house of God. But so it is, that Christ neither by his own commandment, nor by direction of his Spirit inspiring the Apostles, instituted any other day but the Lord's Day. If there had been any other days dedicated to Christ, the Apostle spoke unproperly and obscurely when he said, he was ravished in the spirit upon the Lord's Day. If there had been a day for his Nativity, another for his passion, he should have said, he was ravished in the Spirit upon one of the Lord's Days. Seeing John outlived the rest of the Apostles, It followeth that there was no other holy day observed in the Apostolical times. Neither was the institution of the Lord's Day so much a new institution, as a change of the ordinary Sabbath. The extraordinary Sabbaths were in every respect ceremonial. The ordinary Sabbath had both substance and ceremony. By reason of the substance it was changed into the Lord's Day answering analogically to it. The moral use of the ordinary Sabbath was for the service of God in general both private and public. The mystical use was to be a memorial of things bypast, and a shadow of things to come. The moral use endureth, the mystical uses are evanished. Christ appeared the first day of the week, and every eighth day thereafter until he ascended, saith[2] Junius.

---

[1] Defence of the ceremonies pag. 64
[2] *In Genesin c.* 2:2

And that therefore the Apostles delivered to the Kirk the observation of this day from Christ's example and institution, which he confirmeth with the judgment of Cyrillus and Augustine. The blessing of the seventh day was translated to this day instituted by Christ, because all sanctification floweth to Christians from Christ. But it is sufficient that the Apostles inspired by his Spirit, have recommended this day to the Kirk.

There is another reason to prove that there were no other days appointed in the Apostle's times. The Apostle had occasions to treat of holy days, reasoning against the observation of Jewish days, they direct them to no other as the purpose required. The Apostle condemneth not only the observation of the Jewish days, nor the Jewish observation of the Jewish days to a typical use. For the converted Jews did not observe them as shadows of things to come, for then they had denied Christ: but he condemneth observation of days as a Jewish custom and rite, as a pedagogical and rudimentary instruction not beseeming the Christian Kirk. Zanchius[1] speaketh to this purpose after this manner: *Magis consentaneum est cum prima institutione & cum scriptis Apostolicis ut unus tantum dies in septimana sanctisicetur.* It is more agreeable to the first institution, and the writings of the Apostles, that one day of the week only be sanctified.

Against this Argument is first alleged, that the Apostle compareth with the observation of days, *Romans 14:5,6*. *Answer.* The Apostle beareth with the infirmity of the weak Jews, who understood not the fullness of the Christian liberty. And the ceremonial law was as yet not buried. But the same Apostle reproveth the Galatians, who had attained to this liberty, and had once left off the observation of days. Next, the Judaical days had once that honor, as to be appointed by God himself: but the anniversary days appointed by men have not the like honor.

---

[1] *In 4. praecept. p. 171*

It is secondly objected, that seeing the Lord's Day was instituted in remembrance of Christ's resurrection, the other notable acts of Christ ought likewise to be remembered with their several festivities. Answer. It followeth not that because Christ did institute in remembrance of one benefit, therefore men may institute for other benefits. 2. Christ's resurrection was a benefit including the rest, as an accomplishment of the work of redemption, and answered anagogically [allegorically] to the common benefit of creation by the beginning of a new creation. 3. We deny that the Lord's Day was appointed to celebrate the memory only of Christ's resurrection. For then the Lord's resurrection, the proper subject of all Homilies, Sermons, Gospels, Epistles, Collects, Hymns and Psalms belonging to the Paschal service should be the proper subject of divine service every Lord's Day. Then the Lord's Day should be a festival day: and it were unlawful to fast on it. It was instituted for the remembrance of all his actions, and generally for his worship. Athanasius, saith[1] *In Sabatho conuenimus ut Dominum Sabathi Jesum adoremus.* We convene on the Sabbath, that we may adore Jesus the Lord of the Sabbath. Augustine[2] saith *Dominus hic dies ideirco dicitur, quia eo die Dominus resurrexit, vel ut ipso nomine doceret illus Domino consecratum esse debere.* It is called the Lord's Day, because the Lord rose that day, or that the name might teach us, that it ought to be consecrate to the Lord. It is called the Lord's Day, either because the Lord did institute it: as the days of Purim are called Mordecai's days, in the second of the Maccabees, and the communion is called the Lord's Supper: Or else because it was instituted to the Lord's honor and worship. The Jewish Sabbath was the Sabbath of the Lord our God. The Christian Sabbath is the Sabbath of Christ our Lord, God and Man. The name of Lord was more frequent in the mouths of Christians in the Apostolic times, then the name of

---

[1] *Homilia de semente*
[2] *De verbis Apostol. serm.* 15

Christ as Rhenanus[1] hath observed. When it is called commonly the Lord's Day, it is all one, as if it were commonly called Christ's Day, changing the title but not the purpose. If the ordinary Sabbath be Christ's Day appointed by himself or his Apostles at his direction, for the remembrance of all his actions, and for his worship in general; to divide his actions, and appoint anniversary and mystical days for their remembrance, is superstitious will-worship, and a Judaical addition to Christ's institution. Christ's Day answereth analogically to the moral Sabbath. It may be applied to the remembrance of Christ's resurrection seeing he rose that day and in some sort to be a sign of the heavenly rest. But that is *typus communis & factus*. A common type fitted to resemble such things: But not *typus distinctus* appointed by God for that end. It resteth then that Christ's Day, or the Lord's Day is the Christian Sabbath, a continuation of the moral Sabbath, and to be observed in a moral manner for all the praise of God's worship in and through Christ, and not in a mystical manner, for the joyful remembrance of Christ resurrection only.

It is thirdly objected that Paul kept the feast of Pentecost, *Acts 20 & 1 Corinthians 16*. I answer. It was the Jewish Pentecost, whereof mention is made in these places, Paul needed not to have traveled to Jerusalem, for he might have observed the Christian Pentecost every where Bellarmine himself will not be so bold as to affirm that it was the Christian Pentecost, Francolinus[2] putteth it out of doubt, and saith, it is against the common exposition of the interpreters, for saith he, *Tunc temporis non erant celebres christianorum festivitates cum Euangelium non esset ad huc plenè promulgatum*, the festivities of Christians, were not as yet celebrated, for the Gospel was not yet fully published.

It is fourthly objected out of the Epistles of Polycarp & Polycrates, extant in the history of Eusebius and out of Beda following Eusebius, that the Apostles kept the feast of Easter.

---

[1] *In Tertul. de corona militis*
[2] *De horis canonicis cap.* 84

Answer. Beda was but a fabler, and a follower of fabulous reports: Eusebius was little better treading unknown footsteps, as himself confesseth in the beginning of his story. The Epistles alleged are counterfeit: for it is said in these Epistles that John was a Priest and bear on his forehead the Patalum that is the golden plate like that of the high Priests, *Exodus 37:36*. But no man will grant, saith Scaliger,[1] *Neutrum concedit, quisciverit nullam Christi Apostolum sacerdotem fuisse, & nulli preterquam Summo Sacerdoti Petalon gestare licuisse*. That either John or James bear it, who understand that none of Christ's Apostles was a priest: and that it was lawful to none, but the high priest to bear the golden plate. And yet these Epistles are the eldest records that Eusebius can ground upon. The Bishop of Ely in his sermon taketh needless pains to prove the antiquity of Easter. But when he proveth it to be Apostolical, he shooteth short. His eldest antiquity is the counterfeit Epistles before alleged. His proof out of scripture *Psalm 118:8 & 1 Corinthians 5:7,8* are very weak. For the first testimony is applied to every Lord's Day, and is not to be restrained to Pasche day. Christ crucified and refused of the builders was demonstrate[d] to be the corner stone. For that day he was demonstrate[d] to be the Son of God by his resurrection according to David's Prophecy, Today have I begotten thee, applied to the resurrection by the Apostle, *Acts 13:33*.

The Lord's Day is the day that the Lord hath created, let us exult and rejoice in it. Christ instituted it; David prophesied of it, *Psalm 110* where it is called the day of the Lord's Assemblies. Many memorable things were done under the Old Testament upon this day, to declare that it should be an excellent day under the New Testament, specially Circumcision was commanded on the eight day as a sacrament of that day, saith Junius,[2] *Quia Sacramentum fuit diei illius octavi quo dominus Jesus Christus resurrexit*, following in this conceit the Ancients, Cyprian, Ambrose &c. If it be true

---

[1] *Elenth. Triheres.* c. 25
[2] *In Genes.* 17:12

that is affirmed by the Council of Constantinople[1] it would appear that the Lord hath of purpose heaped his wonderful works upon this day: for there it is said that Christ was born on it: The star shined to the wise men on it: Christ fed 5000 with 5 loaves and 2 fishes on it: Christ was baptized on it, rose on it, sent down the Holy Ghost on it: on it the light was created, Pope Leo likewise saith, *Dies dominica tantis dispensationum mysteriis est consecrata, ut quicquid insigne admodum est constitutum in terris, in hujus diei dignitatem sit gestum: id est.* that the Lord's Day is consecrate[d] with so many mysteries dispensed on it, that it appeareth that whatsoever potable thing was done on earth, was done to the honor of this day. So if the prophecy of David should be applied to any precise day, it should be applied to the Lord's Day. But seeing the words are to be understood, as well of David as of Christ, the day is taken for the time indefinitely, wherein David was made King, and the Corner Stone of God's people. The other testimony importeth not the celebration of Easter feast upon any anniversary day, but rather the Apostle teacheth us to celebrate this feast of the Passover all the year long, with the unleavened bread of sincerity and truth. Doctor Fulk in his answer to the Rhemists upon the same place citeth Augustine, referring this feasting not to the celebration of Easter, nor to the receiving of Pasche communion, but to our whole life. It is therefore only the Bishop's conjecture that the incestuous person was cut of against the feast of Easter, that a little leaven might not leaven the whole lump. His last proof is taken from the custom of baptism and the Eucharist ministered upon Pasche day, as if they had been ministered only on that day. It was the decree of Pope Innocentius in the Lateran Council that all should communicate at Easter. The Christian Sabbath was called the Lord's Day, the day of light, and the day of Bread. The day of light because of baptism ministered ordinarily on the Lord's

---

[1] *Conc. Constant 6. Can. 8*

Day: for the Ancients called baptism, Light, or illumination. The day of bread because of the administration of the Supper ordinarily upon the Lord's Day, as Junius[1] proveth out of Chrysostome baptism was tied of old to Pentecost, as well as Easter. It was an evil custom disallowed both by ancient and modern Divines. It was not so in the Primitive Kirk, as Cassander beareth witness.[2] *Apostolorum doctrinae consentientes nullo temporum aut locorum delectu statim post fidei professionem ab Apostolis vel Apostolorum discipulis baptismi sacramento in Ecclesiam Christi captabantur.* I will now frame an argument against this conceit of Apostolical tradition and observation of Pasche. The Apostles were led all their lifetime by the infallible direction of the Spirit. If they had accorded on the observation of Easter they had not disagreed on the day. But their most ancient records, the bastard Epistles above mentioned report that Philip and John kept the fourteenth day of the moon, as the Jews did, and Peter the Lord's Day following the fourteenth day of the moon. It is well said in the preface to the harmony of confessions; that the old contention about the celebrating of Easter tossed very hotly the space of two hundred years or thereabout, betwixt the Greeks and the Latins, was long since of us thought worthy of laughter. Whitaker saith,[3] *Magnam quidem de hoc re olim fuisse contentione sed sine causa: ut miru sit de re tantilla, et pene nullius momenti tantas et tam graves fuisse dissentiones,* wondering at their frivolous contention. The golden number invented to find out the new moon, for observing the right day, after that they accorded upon one day hath often failed, and notwithstanding of all the rules set down by the Council of Nice for uniformity in keeping the day, it hath been differently observed through mistaking, as Bellarmine himself[4] confesseth. So God suffered the Christian world to

---

[1] *In Genesin c. 2*
[2] *Expositio de author. consue. bapti Infant. adulti*
[3] *De scriptura quaest. 6 c. 9*
[4] *De cultis Sanctorum. c.12*

wander, notwithstanding of their golden number; to let the world see such customs had not his allowance. He suffered not the Jews to wander in such incertainties, after he had appointed them unto the keeping of their Passover.

Lastly, they reason with Augustine,[1] *a posteriori*, that seeing the Lord's Passion, Resurrection, Ascension, & coming down of the Holy Ghost, is celebrated with anniversary solemnity, through all the world, they must needs have been ordained either by the Apostles, or by general Councils. But so it is, that those days were solemnly kept before there was any general Council. It must follow therefore that the Apostles ordained them. *Answer*. Augustine's dis-junction is not necessary: For many customs crept in, and prevailed thereafter universally, which were neither ordained by the Apostles, nor general Councils. Socrates in his History saith,[2] I am of opinion, that as many other things crept in of custom in sundry places, so the feast of Easter to have prevailed among all people of a certain private custom and observation: insomuch that not one of the Apostles hath any where prescribed so much as one rule of it to any man. The success & event hath manifestly declared unto the world, that of old it was observed, not of Canon, but of custom. And a little after, They that keep Easter the 14th day of the month, bring forth John the Apostle for their Author. Such as inhabit Rome, and the West parts of the world, allege Peter and Paul for themselves, that they should leave such a tradition: yet there is none of them that can shew in writing any testimony of theirs for confirmation and proof of that custom. Thus far Socrates translated by Doctor Hanmer a formalist,[3] for answer to Augustine's rule. In the days of Justin Martyr, that is, in the midst of the second age after the Apostles, there is no mention made of any other holy day then the Lord's Day. In his second Apology he seemeth to affirm, that the Christians had only two times of public

---

[1] *Epist.* 118
[2] *Lib.* 5. c. 22
[3] See farther in Socrates in the same chapter.

meetings: the one ordinary upon the Lord's Day: the other extraordinary and uncertain, viz. when any was converted to the Christian faith, and baptized. As for the questions extant among Justin's works, the learned do not acknowledge them for his. In Augustine's rule there is no mention of the nativity day. As for the other four days mentioned, put the case they were universally observed in Augustine's time, that is, in the fifth age after the Apostles, yet except they were perpetually observed, Augustine's rule will not help them. If they cannot prove Pasche to be Apostolical, how will they prove the Pentecost, the Passion, Ascension day to be Apostolical? There is Sermons extant amongst Cyprians works upon the Passion and Ascension days. But Bellarmine himself confesseth these Sermons of Christ's cardinal works to be[1] suppositions. The observing of the passion day brought into the Kirk, set days of fasting, the Friday fast, Lenten fast, and a number of superstitions accompanying the said fastings together with the opinion of merit by fasting. Set anniversary fasts are condemned by our Divines. The right manner of fasting is to fast when some judgment is imminent, some great work to be performed. And as for the private man, when he is greatly tempted to sin, and cannot overcome his tentation [temptation], then is it fittest time for him to fast. The Paschal fasts were also abused for the Paschal communion following, as if Easter communion required greater preparation then any other communion in the year.

The sixth Reason.

If it had been the will of God, that the several acts of Christ should have been celebrate[d] with several solemnities, the Holy Ghost would have made known to us the day of his Nativity, Circumcision, presentation to the Temple, Baptism, Transfiguration, and the like. For it is kindly to remember

---

[1] *De scriptoribus Ecclesiasticis. pag.* 93

Opus diei in die sua, the work of the day in the own day. This was the custom of old under the Law. Hooker saith, That the wondrous works of God advanced the days & times, wherein they were wrought. Bellarmine saith, That Christ's acts did consecrate the days and times wherein they were wrought. If the principal works of God advance some days above other, all the days of the year should be holy. If we should honor the memory of Christ's acts, all days likewise should be holy, because every one of them is full of his miracles, as he saith,[1] Christ by his actions did no more consecrate the times wherein they were wrought, than his body did the Manger, or the Cross. Not Christ's action on a day, but his institution maketh a day holy. If Christ's actions advance & consecrate the days whereon they were wrought, the days ought to be known. Otherwise it will fall out that we shall keep the days holy that were never advanced nor consecrated either by Christ's action or institution. But so it is, that the day of Christ nativity, and consequently the other days depending upon the calculation of the same, is hid from mortal men. That Christ was born the 25th day of December, is grounded upon an erroneous conceit that Zachary the father of John Baptist was an high Priest, when as he was a Priest of one of the 24 orders, that is, of the order of Abijah. The Ancients made John the Baptist to be conceived the 24th of September, when Zachary as high Priest should have offered up incense. And from the conception of John they counted six full months to the conception of Christ, that is, to the 25th of March, when as they should have counted but five full months. This opinion of Christ's nativity on the 25th day of December was bred at Rome. Scaliger saith,[2] *Post seculum Constantini, Romae haec observatio instituta & tempore Chrysostomi Constantinopolin derivata est*, that this observation was instituted at Rome after Constantine's time. Chrysostom in his Homilies upon the Nativity saith, That ten years ago before the making of the

---

[1] *Epistol. 4 c. 4*
[2] *De emendat temporum lib. 6*

said Homily, the 25th day of December, was made known to the Oriental Kirks by the Occidental [Western], to have been the day of Christ's Nativity. Epiphanius testifieth, that he was ignorant, that the Occidental Kirk had ordained the 25th day of December to have been the day of the Lord's nativity, a little before he made his book against heresies. All the Kirks of the East, and of Egypt, observed one day, for the nativity and baptism of Christ upon the Epiphany day. Ambrose is the most ancient, who maketh mention of the 25th day of December,[1] saith Scaliger. The diversity of the Ancients observing some the 6th of January, some the 19th of April, some the 19th of May, some the 25th of December, argueth that the Apostles never ordained it. Bellarmine nor no other can produce a writer for 300 years to testify that the Nativity day was kept. Clemens Constitutions are known to be counterfeit and late, as Scaliger proveth in the same place. Because they make mention of the 25th day of December which was not received in his time, namely, in the Oriental Kirk. By the same argument may the counterfeit Epistle of Theophilus be rejected, for it maketh likewayes [likewise] the nativity to fall on the 25th day of December, as a matter out of all doubt. Cyprians sermon on the Nativity is acknowledg[ed] by Bellarmine himself to be suppositious, as I have said before. Ye se then as God hid the body of Moses, so hath he hid this day and other days depending on the calculation of it, wherein he declared his will concerning the other days of his notable acts. To wit that not Christ's action but Christ's institution maketh a day holy. Bellarmine saith,[2] *Dies dominica refert nobis memoriam natalis Christi et resurrectionis ejusdem, et adventus Spirit us Sancti, nam Christ us die dominica nat us est*, Christ was borne upon the Lord's Day. If this be true, what needeth us an anniversary day after a Jewish manner. They will not suffer the ordinary Sabbath, that is Christ's Day, serve in a moral manner for unknown days: but they will set up a

---

[1] *Canon Isagog. lib. 3. Pag.* 301
[2] *De cultis Sanctorum cap.* 11

mystical day uncertain and unknown, and equal it with the Lord's Day, that is, the true Christ's Day institute[d] by himself. Why should we follow antiquity blinded in this point, & foster a gross error of Zacharius high priesthood against the express word of God? He was a Priest of the eighth order: every order kept their course and station about the Temple from Sabbath to Sabbath, *1 Chronicles 9:25*. None of them encroached upon others, but kept the order set down by David and to that effect was made a severe Canon, Every Priest or Levite, that meddled with the function of another let him die the death as Scaliger reporteth out of their ancient laws[1] *Omnis sive Sacerdos sive Levita qui sese immiseuerit function alterius, capite luat*. This order was so observed, that if any of the 24 families had failed either by famine or by the sword, the daily sacrifice ceased in the time of their function, and no other family would supply the room. But from the instauration [restoration] and dedication made by Judas Maccabeus the 22nd day of November, when the first family began to keep their Station, there was no intermission of the daily sacrifice, no interruption of the courses, till the destruction of the Temple, as Scaliger proveth in the end of his[2] book. By the calculation from the 22nd of November at the dedication made by Maccabeus, he maketh John the Baptist to be conceived after the 28th day of July, and consequently Christ's birth to fall out about the end of September, an hot time of the year, when the Shepherds were watching in the field. Casaubon[3] saith, That the custom of the Kirk of Alexandria doth wonderfully confirm the calculation of Scaliger. The day of the week when Christ was borne, can no mortal man know, saith the same[4] Scaliger. They who were of one family divided the services among themselves, as it fell by lot: some fell to offer Incense, some to dress the lamps,

---

[1] *Canon Isagog. lib. 3. pag. 298*
[2] *De emendat temporum*
[3] *Exercit. 1. pag. 163*
[4] *Canon Isagog. lib. 3 pag. 300*

some to order the wood on the Altar, *1 Chronicles 23:28-31*. And the book of the Jewish Liturgies testifies the same. So you see how it fell Zachary to offer up incense, and that he was not high Priest. If antiquity erred so grossly in the matter itself, that is, in taking the 25th day of December for the day of Christ's nativity, might they not have erred as grossly in appointing any day at all? Nay let us utter the truth, December-Christmas is a just imitation of the December-Saturnal of the Ethnick Romans, and so used as if Bacchus, and not Christ were the God of Christians.

It is commonly objected, that we may as well keep a day for the nativity as for the resurrection of Christ. We have answered already, that Christ's Day or the Lord's Day, is the day appointed for remembrance of his nativity, and all his actions and benefits, as well as for the resurrection. Next, the one is moral and weekly: the other is mystical and anniversary. The Lord's Day itself is no longer to us mystical, but moral, saith[1] Willet: and therefore Pasche-day is a mystical Sabbath, and anniversary: whereas the Lord's Sabbath should be only moral.

It is still objected, the benefits of God ought to be remembered, specially Christ's notable benefits. *Answer.* It is one thing to remember, another thing to remember with solemn festivities. To remember is a moral duty and perpetual: for we ought to keep not only an anniversary, but also a weekly and daily remembrance. But to celebrate an anniversary solemnity, and to keep a Sabbath of rest in remembrance, it is a pedagogical ceremony of the Jews. The Lord helped their understanding with types and figures, their affections with instruments of Music, their memories with frontlets and Phylacteries to put them in mind of God's Law. But we are to keep saith Jerome[2] not a literal by outward signs, but a spiritual memory of God's law. Everything set up for remembrance of God is not acceptable to him: for so the

---

[1] *Synops pap* of holy daies
[2] *Ad Celanthiam Epist.* 14. c. 1

Lutheran shall defend his images. As oft as the Gospel is preached, Christ is remembered. When the word is preached, Christ is crucified, and by the same reason, he may be said to be born, to rise again, to ascend, &c. When the sacrament is ministered, Christ's death and Passion is remembered, and that with solemnity. We cannot worship Christ privately or publicly, but we must remember his birth and his passion. Pope Alexander III[1] gave this reason, wherefore the Roman Kirk kept not a holy day to the Trinity, *Quoniam Ecclesia Romana in usu non habet quod in aliquo tempore buiusmodi celebret specialiter festivitatem: cum singulis diebus gloria Patri & filio, & Spiritui Sancto, & coetera simitia dicantur ad laudem pertinentia Trenitalis.* Because, saith he, Glory to the Father, and to the Son, and to the Holy Ghost, and other such like things belonging to the praise of the Trinity, are uttered daily. The Pope's reason is grounded upon this rule. Whatsoever is entreated or remembered in the ordinary divine service, ought not to have one special holy day to celebrate the memory of the same, beside the day already discerned by the Lord. We assume, Christ's nativity, death, resurrection, &c. are not only the continual meditation of a Christian in private; but also are remembered, and entreated in the ordinary and public service. Every communion Sunday is a passion holy day. Every Sabbath that Christ's nativity is preached, is a time of remembrance of his Nativity. But to ordain an anniversary day, or hour of rest for commemoration of his nativity, or passion, and specially upon a week day is a Jewish rudiment, and a prejudice to Christian liberty.

As for the 5th day of November it is not an holy day. It is not a day of cessation from work, which is one of the chief elements of an holy day. The bonfires set out in token of joy are no part of Christian sanctification of the day. Bellarmine telleth us,[2] *Ignis accendi solet ad letitiam significandam etiam in rebus prophanis*, that fire useth to be kindled, even in civil and

---

[1] *Decreta lib. 2. Tit. 9, cap*
[2] *De reliquijs c. 4*

profane things. Scaliger[1] calleth the candles and torches lightened upon Midsummer even, the foot steps of ancient gentility. Anniversary commemoration of a benefit, with a cessation from work, suppose for a part of a day is Jewish. To praise God with public thanksgiving in the instant time of receiving the benefit was our duty, but to appoint an anniversary hour of cessation and public commemoration, is not competent to the times of the New Testament. Willet compareth this day to the days of Purim. Be it so, but these days were of a ceremonial nature, as we have said.

The seventh Reason.

Grant the keeping of holy days to have been at the beginning a matter indifferent, and setting aside all the former reasons, yet ought they to be abolished, because according to the rule of the Fathers, commended to us by Zanchius, *Non malè igitur fecerunt qui omnia praeter diem Dominicum aboleverunt*,[2] Things indifferent, when they are abused and polluted with superstition, ought to be abolished. In this rank he placeth holidays, and therefore inferreth, that they have not done evil, who have abolished all other holidays but the Lord's Day. When he saith, They have not done evil, it is all one as if he had said, They had done well: for they have done according to that laudable rule. Sure it is, that in former times holidays have not only been abused to idleness and licentiousness, but also polluted with the opinion of worship, merit, necessity, and Judaical conceit, that the Devil did not tempt on these days, as he did on other days. Therefore the same Zanchius saith in the place aforesaid, If any feasts were celebrate before religiously and holily, but thereafter were contaminate with superstition and Idolatry,[3] that worthily they were taken away by our Reformers, who imitate herein

---

[1] *De Emendat tempor. lib. 7. pag.* 713
[2] In 4. praecept. Col. 678
[3] Col. 678

the example of Hezekiah's bruising to powder the brazen Serpent when it was abused to idolatry. And again he saith, The number, the abuses, the superstitions, the false worships, the will-worships of feasts so increased, that there is nothing in the Kirk so unsavory to God,[1] so pernicious to men, as to sanctify such and so many days. We pretend that we place no part of God's worship in the observation of days. But how can we observe a day to the honor of Christ, and not worship him by that observation? That were to make his honor no honor. We use to reason against the Papists after this manner. To dedicate days to Saints is religious worship. Is it not then religious worship to dedicate a day to Christ? Yea surely, and will-worship. And so they were not only polluted with will-worship, but are at this hour of themselves a mere will-worship.

The 8th Reason.

That which lawfully hath been abolished by civil and Ecclesiastical laws, and by consent and uniform practice in the contrary without interruption, and beyond the prescription of time allowed to things moveable (put the case holy days were things moveable, and indifferent) and hath been borne down by sermons of all the most reverent Preachers since the reformation, corrected with censures, and abjured by public oaths of Preachers and professors, cannot lawfully be received, and put in practice again. Hooker and Saravia urged for maintenance of their ceremonies, Law, custom, prescription, and craveth that the impiety and unlawfulness of their ceremonies be proved; or else that the non-conformists conform. May we not plead after the same manner for our former order so long established, and that they prove it was impious, and unlawful before we make a change? And so much the rather, because we have sworn. Our

---

[1] See farther in Zanchius in Coloss 2

oath by itself bindeth more then Law, custom, and prescription: far more when it concurreth with them. The assumption is evident by that which I have already set down in the beginning. If Zanchius approved the abolition of holy days in some Kirks where they were, because they have been polluted and grossly abused: much more would he and other divines knowing the truth of our case think it unlawful to reinduce them amongst us.

The judgment of the Reformed Kirks.

Of the ancient Kirks I have spoken before. Some excuse the Ancients with good intention, because to win the Gentiles they converted their days into Christian holy days. Others excused them with the circumstance of time, that dwelling among Pagans, they made profession before their eyes of Christ's birth, Passion, resurrection &c. by observing such days. But the wisdom of their intention has proven folly, as the 7th reason maketh manifest. The like circumstance of time is not offered: Therefore we may not be excused. It is gross ignorance to say that holy days were so many hundred years before Papistry. For Papistry hath been in the Kirk ever since the days of the Apostles: yea the mystery of iniquity was working in their times. The errors of the Orthodox Kirk were the beginnings of Papistry, at length they grew to a great mass. So howbeit the whole lump was not formed, till the Antichrist came to his full strength, yet many particulars were entered before, and like brooks came into the great river. As the Antichrist was borne and did grow in years, so did Papistry. As for the reformed Kirks, except our neighbor Kirk, they have abandoned days dedicate to Saints. Some admit days dedicate to Christ, some two, some five: But not with the full consent and good liking of the learned, But either forced by the authority of the Magistrate, or willfulness of the people, or because remaining in the midst of their enemies, they are not permitted otherwayes [otherwise] to do. Farrel and Viret removed all holy days out of the Kirk of Geneva, as Calvin testifies. The same decree which banished Farel and Calvin out of Geneva brought in other holy days.[1] They were all again abrogate[d] except the Sabbath day. Howsoever after came in the keeping of Pasche and the Nativity. Calvin was so far from liking of holy days, that he was slandered of intention to abolish the Lord's Day. The Belgic Kirks in their Synod holden at Dordt *Anno* 1578 wished, that only the Lord's Day might be celebrate[d]. Yea Luther himself in his book *de bonis operibus*, set forth *Anno* 1520 wished that there were no feast days among Christians, but the Lord's Day. And in his book to the Nobility of Germany, he saith, *Consultum esse ut omnia festa aboleantur, solo Dominico die retento.* It were expedient that all feast days were abrogate[d], the Lord's Day only retained. Howsoever foreign divines in their Epistles & Councils speak sometime sparingly against holy days, when their advice was sought of Kirks newly risen out of Popery, and greatly distressed: they never advised a Kirk to resume them where they were removed, neither had they leisure to consider narrowly the corruption of every error, that prevailed in their time, the work of reformation was so painful to them. I wish therefore that the judicious Reader would ponder the reasons set down in this treatise. As for our neighbor Kirk standing in the midst betwixt the Roman and reformed Kirks as Bucer once said is more liberal in their feasts,[2] as in other ceremonies, then the other reformed Kirks as Gretzerus the Jesuit hath observed.[3] *Calvino-Papistae Angli ut in aliis quae ad ritus et ceremonias pertinent, longe liberaliores sunt quam puritani in Gallia, Germania, Belgia: ita et in festis retinendis longe largiores.* They observe not only the five holy days already mentioned, but other days also dedicate[d] to Christ. The feast of circumcision was not remembered in the Calendars, but within this 500th year. Nazianzen is the first

---

[1] *Epist.* 118
[2] Brightman. In *Apocalypsen. cap.* 3.
[3] *De festis lib.* 1. *c.* 2

that maketh mention of the Epiphany day. Neither was it institute at the first for the wise men. There is no homily of any farther extent for the feast of purification before the days of Justinian. The feast of the Trinity was not kept at Rome itself in the days of Alexander the 3rd. They keep also a number of Saints days: so that their days in number are more, then the Jews themselves observed. The reasons already alleged against days dedicate[d] to Christ, may serve also against days dedicate[d] to Saints and Angels. We may look assuredly that the five days presently urged will bring in all the rest, to make up our Conformity with our neighbor Kirk, which to us is not lawful. They were never removed from amongst them: we have abandoned and abjured them. If the Apostle reproved the Galatians so sharply that beginning in the spirit, they returned to the flesh, that is to the ceremonies of Moses' Law, some time ordained by God, what reproof deserve we after we have begun in the Spirit, and run so well, and so long, if we return to human traditions & superstitions. To conclude then, to esteem one day above another in respect of any mystery certainly known, or commonly reputed to have been wrought upon that day. To testify this estimation by cessation from work. To devise a particular service to be done upon it accounting that form or part of service acceptable to God, because it is performed on that day: is to observe a day: and in this manner do we observe anniversary days. The same consideration may be applied to an anniversary hour.

Of Confirmation

Imposition of hands, was a ceremony used in personal prayers and blessings before the Law, under the Law, and under the Gospel, Jacob imposed hands on the sons of Joseph when he blessed them, *Genesis 48*. Moses laid his hand upon Joshua his successor; *Numbers 27*. The elders that were admitted to be Councilors in the great Sanhedrin, were admitted with imposition of hands. The Rabbins were promoved [promoted] to their high degree of doctorship, by imposition of hands. In the New Testament we read, that Christ laid on hands on the children whom he blessed; *Matthew 19:13*. The Apostles gave the gifts of tongues, Prophesying, and working of miracles, by imposition of hands: *Acts 8*. The faithful indued with the gift of healing, and casting out devils, laid on hands on the persons cured, *Mark 14*. Office-bearers in the Kirk were received with imposition of hands, *Acts 6 & 1 Timothy 4*. Paul and Barnabas when they were sent forth in a special embassage, were commended to the grace of God by imposition of hands: *Acts 13*. When the Catechumenists were thoroughly catechized, they were admitted to the society of the communicants by imposition of hands, *Hebrews 6*.

Imposition of hands used in so divers actions, civil and religious, was no Sacrament, for who will admit, that the inauguration of Magistrates and Doctors, or admission of rulers to be Councilors, is a sacrament? It was only a simple rite, and sign of limitation or restraint, specifying, or setting forth, the party, on whom we desire God to pour his blessing: that is, it was only an indicant and demonstrative sign of the person on whom the blessing was poured, and not a significant or declarative sign of the blessing or grace itself bestowed. A signification may indeed be devised, as some devise this analogy betwixt it and the thing signified; that the imposition of the hand, doth in some sort resemble the hand of God stretched forth for the protecting, assisting, and safe keeping, of the party: and so it may be *signum factum*, a sign, made and accommodate[d] to signify such a thing: but it is not *signum destinatum*, a sign instituted by God to signify such a thing, for we have no warrant for such a signification in all the Scripture.

The imposition of hands mentioned, *Acts 8* was not ordinary, but extraordinary and temporary. The Apostles gave the extraordinary gifts, of tongues, prophecy, and such like, for they were seen of them that stood by, and served for a general confirmation of the truth of their doctrine. The gift of sanctification and strength against all temptations of sin, and assaults of the Devil, is a grace invisible, serving for the confirmation of every Christian in particular, and bestowed only upon the faithful; whereas the former gifts called *gratiae gratis datae* by the Schoolmen, might have been bestowed upon persons unsanctified, this place maketh[1] nothing for confirmation. The confession of Wurtemberg hath these words, Of a temporal and personal fact of the Apostles, a general and perpetual sacrament cannot be ordained in the Kirk without a special command of God. By the Spirit then bestowed, is meant, not the sanctifying Spirit, but the extraordinary gifts of the Spirit: for no doubt the Spirit was given when Philip preached and baptized, except we will believe that the Eunuch was baptized by Philip without the Spirit.[2] *Nisi fortè Eunuchus à Philippo Diacono sine Spiritu sancto baptizatus fuisse credendus est*. Peter and John bestowed the spirit in another manner, to wit, in an extraordinary manner: These extraordinary gifts of the Spirit are called simply the Spirit, not only in this place, but also *Acts 19* and *John 7*. The Spirit was not, because Christ was not as yet glorified.

---

[1] *Cap.* 11
[2] *Hieron advers. Lucifer.*

The Imposition of hands mentioned, *Hebrews 6:2* is exponed [expounded] by Theophilactus to be that wonderful imposition of hands by the which they received the Spirit to prophesy and work miracles. Others expone it to be the imposition of hands ordinatory, or consecratory of Ministers in their office. A third sort take it for an ordinary and common rite, whereby the catechized were initiate[d], and entered into the society of the communicants. Let this third interpretation be admitted as the greatest ground of confirmation, it will not serve their turn. The Apostle opponeth [opposes] the doctrine of the beginning, that is, the catechetical doctrine of repentance from dead works, faith, and resurrection of the dead, and eternal judgment, to the doctrine of perfection. The Catechumenists were either Infidels of perfect age, converted to the faith, or else the children of Christians come to perfect age. The first sort were tried of their sufficient knowledge in the Catechetical doctrine, before they were baptized and admitted to the communion. The second sort were tried before they were admitted amongst the number of communicants. They were before in *Ecclesia foederatorum*, in the Kirk of the covenant: they entered in *Ecclesiam adultorum* into the society of the elder sort, after trial of their sufficient knowledge, by a recommendation of the Kirk; the ceremony whereof was imposition of hands.[1] The ancient Kirk received penitents within the bosom of the Kirk by imposition of hands: and it was called *Impositio manuum reconciliatoria*. Siclike [suchlike] Heretics and Schismatics were received with imposition of[2] hands. And this was done before the[3] communion: whereby we may see that imposition of hands was nothing else but a gesture of personal prayer, and blessing, whereby they entered or re-entered into the society of the communicants. Bellarmine[4] acknowledgeth that the

---

[1] *Beza antithesis papismi & christianismi c. 70. Zanchius & Pareus in Hebrews 6*
[2] *Concil Arelat. c. 8*
[3] *Conail. Laod. c. 7*
[4] *De confirmat. c. 7*

imposition of hands reconciliatory, was not a consecration imprinting a character; but a ceremony furthering prayer, or a prayer upon the person. As it was nothing else but a gesture of prayer in the re-entry, so was it only a gesture of prayer in the entry. The reformed Kirks observe the same order in admitting to the Lord's table, either the children of Christians, or strangers from other parts: they admit them not but with prayers, and after due examination of their knowledge, and personal profession of the known truth. The Kirk of Scotland at the first reformation ordained, that children should be examined for the first time, at the ninth year of their age; for the second, at the twelfth; for the third at the fourteenth: & since hath practiced continual examination in the Catechetical doctrine, with prayers reiterate, for their growth in knowledge and Sanctification; and without sufficient trial they were not admitted to the Lord's table. And this was thought sufficient, to unite the baptized with the society of the communicants. The gesture of imposition of hands other reformed Kirks, and ours also, have omitted: because it was a rite indifferent: for it was but an indicant sign of the person admitted: and because it hath been, and is still abused to make up a bastard Sacrament; the Sacrament of confirmation, which we have condemned, not only in the confession of faith, but also in the confession of Helvetia approved in the general Assembly holden at Edinburgh *Anno* 1566. And thirdly, because this gesture of personal prayer is omitted in other cases, as reconciling of Penitents, Schismatics, and Converts, even where Confirmation is used, that the world may see, it is not used by them in confirmation as a gesture of personal prayer and blessing, but to a further intent.

 Imposition of hands was not called *Confirmation* until it was turned into a sacrament. This name of *Confirmation* was given of old, not only to the action of anointing the forehead of the baptized with chrism [consecrated oil] in the form of a cross:

but also, to the giving of the cup to the communicants[1]. But at this day it is used only in the first sense and howbeit the oily cross be removed, yet the corruptions which came in with it, remain still with the imposition of hands, the only sensible matter, that is, the essence of this Sacrament in the opinion of many Schoolmen.

It is said, that by imposition of hands and prayer, the baptized receive strength and defense against all temptations to sin, and the assaults of the world and the devil, in confirmation. And again, that it is a sign to certify the confirmed of God's favor and gracious goodness toward them is it not then a seal, let be a sign indicant, or a simple gesture of prayer; Bellarmine maketh Imposition of hands and prayer, but one sensible sign in the Sacrament of confirmation, doeth not Mr. Hutton say likewise, that Imposition of hands is one of the external means by the which the Holy Ghost is given? And howbeit that prayer have the chief force, yet Imposition of hands hath some also, otherwise, saith he, What needed Peter and John to have traveled to Samaria? They might have prayed in Jerusalem for the Holy Ghost to the Samaritans.

The grace received in confirmation, is called strength, and defense against all temptations to sin, and the assaults of the world and the devil. In baptism the grace received is for the forgiveness of sins. Do not the papists distinguish after the same manner betwixt baptism and confirmation that the Holy Ghost is given in baptism, to remission of sins, life and Sanctification and in confirmation for force, strength, and corroboration to fight against all our spiritual enemies, and to stand constantly in confession of our faith even to death, in times of persecution, either of the heathen or of heretics, with great increase[2] of grace. Hooker saith,[3] that in baptism infants are admitted to live in God's family, but in confirmation they are enabled to fight in the army of God, and bring forth the

---

[1] *Cassandri liturgica pag.* 228
[2] Rhemists, Acts 8:17
[3] *Ecclesiast. policie. l.* 5, *pag.* 354

fruits of the Holy Ghost. Doctor Hackwell[1] saith that as in baptism they believe remission of sins unto justification, so in confirmation, they are emboldened to make open profession of this belief unto salvation. Doth not his opposition between baptism and confirmation jump just with the opposition made by the Papists who make the principal grace of confirmation, strength to profess the faith in time of persecution? The Papists say, the comforter promised by Christ to his Kirk, was bestowed in the Sacrament of confirmation. Is not the like said in the prayer before Confirmation; The papists say, that in confirmation they receive the seven fold grace of the holy spirit: wisdom, counsel, strength, knowledge, understanding, godliness, fear: is not the like said in the prayer before the laying on of hands; D. Hackwell[2] saith that which the grace of the spirit hath already begun in baptism, is confirmed and perfited [perfected] in confirmation. Is not this just the popish opinion, that he is not a perfite [perfect] Christian who is not confirmed? That Novatus because he was not confirmed, had not all his Christendom: that the unction of confirmation is the perfitting [perfecting] unction. And are not all these oppositions derogations from baptism and the Lord's Supper; Christian valor and courage to resist the devil, and to profess the truth, is it not a part of that life, and Sanctification given in baptism; are not the gifts of the Holy Spirit given after baptism, as a continual performance of the promise of God's assistance sealed up in baptism? In baptism we put on Christ and all his benefits, we enter into God's army as well as into his family, abrenuncing [renouncing] the world and the devil. Concilium Mileuitanum saith, *Qui dicit baptismum in remissionem peccatorum dari tantum, non etiam in adjutorium gratiae anathema sit.* Let him be anathema, who saith that baptism is given to the remission of sins and not to the help of future grace. Chrysostom saith,[3] the baptized was anointed as

---

[1] Serm. of confirmation
[2] Serm. of confirmation
[3] Homil. 6 in Coloss.

one that was to enter into grace. Is not the Lord's Supper the true Sacrament of confirmation of our faith, as well as confirmation of Charity?

If imposition of hands were only a gesture of prayer, for strength, then it might and ought to be reiterate[d] according to Augustine saying,[1] *Manus aute impositio non sicut baptismus repeti non potest quid enim est aliud nisi oratio super hominem.* For we have often need to be strengthened. The Papists say, that impositions of hands in confirmation, is an effectual sign of grace, imprinting an indelible character, and therefore it may not be reiterate[d], neither do they reiterate it.

In the catechism before confirmation, it is said, that there are two only Sacraments generally necessary to salvation. Is there other Sacraments beside howbeit not necessary; Estius[2] saith, that the custom of the universal Kirk, doth prove sufficiently that confirmation is not necessary to salvation; otherwise the godly and careful mother the Kirk, would not neglect to see this sacrament Ministered to the baptized at the point of death.

The Sacrament of confirmation was given of old immediately after baptism to all of whatsoever condition, or estate,[3] even to infants, & when the little ones were confirmed they had godfathers & godmothers, as they have yet in papistical Kirks. Augustine[4] saith, *Quando imposumus manus ist is infantibus altendit unusquisque vestrum utrum linguis loquerentur.* When we laid hands on their infants ye waited whether they would speak with tongues. The Papists themselves will not imitate this toy of antiquity and yet they are little better in deferring confirmation only to the seventh year of their age. Our late act made at the last pretended assembly, ordaineth children of eight years of age to be catechized, and presented to the Bishop to lay hands upon

---

[1] *Lib. 3. de bapt. cap. 16*
[2] *In lib. 4. dist. 7*
[3] *Swarez. tom. 3. disput. 35. sect. 1*
[4] *Tract. 6. in 1. canonicam Johannis*

them. We must be like our neighbors, whether there be reason or no. Is it time to enter the Society of the communicants and doctrine of perfection, as soon as they can rehearse like parrots, a little catechism? We must have god-fathers and god-mothers in confirmation, also well as our neighbors.

When the neoteric [modern] writers speak of confirming the catechized by the rite of Imposition of hands, they take imposition of hands for a sign, of the Kirk confirming them in their possession by her approbation, and not for a sign and seal of the spirit confirming and strengthening.

Of Bishoping

We have abjured Episcopal government, and therefore we cannot lawfully admit Episcopal confirmation, giving and not granting their office were lawful, and that they have gotten a lawful calling by the Kirk to the said office: thirdly that we were free of our oath: and fourthly that confirmation were to be allowed, whether as a ceremony, or as a sacrament, yet it is damnable presumption to appropriate unto themselves the duty that belongeth to all Pastors.

They allege some similitudes for their purpose: it appertaineth to the Captain to take up the role of the soldiers, and furnish them with armor, the shepherd should mark his own sheep &c. As if every Minister were not a Captain in the Lord's Army and a shepherd feeding the flock concredite [entrusted] to him. Bonaventura[1] confesseth, *In talibus nempe rationibus & convenientijs magis locum habet congruitas quam necessitas quia institutio necessitatem facit precipuè*. That there is no necessity, but congruity in such reasons, and that institution chiefly maketh necessity. As for the congruities they agree as well to simple Ministers as to Bishops. Bellarmine himself saith[2] *Non necessario id requirit natura rei quasi aliter sieri non posset, sed quia voluit Dominus hac re honorare episcopalem dignitatem.* That the nature of the thing itself doth not necessarily require it, but only that the Lord will honor Episcopal dignity by it, they are forced therefore to forsake their reasons and congruity as insufficient: and to take them to the will and institution of the Lord.

Our first reason then against them, is, the want of institution or example in the Scripture. They can allege no

---

[1] *In lib. 4. dist. 7. num. 17*
[2] *De confirmatione*

other place [but] *Acts 8* where Peter and John are sent to Samaria to impose hands on those who had been baptized by Philip. If Phillip might have done it, what needed the Apostles to have traveled to Samaria for that purpose? None but Apostles imposed hands: Bishops are the only successors of the Apostles. *Answer*. Giving and not granting that Bishops are the Apostle's successors, first it is untrue that the Apostles only imposed hands, when the Holy Ghost was bestowed: for Ananias laid hands on Paul, *Acts 9:17* he not only cured him of his blindness but also said the Lord hath sent me unto thee, that thou mayest be filled with the Holy Ghost. 2. Peter and John were sent, not only to impose hands, but generally to advance the work begun by Philip. 3. There is no imposition of hands mentioned in that place, but extraordinary, and only extraordinary effects are reckoned, as hath already been said. They exercised this extraordinary power not as Bishops, but as Apostles. Bishops are not their successors in their extraordinary power, for then they might give the gift of tongues and prophesying. 4. Admitting that imposition of hands to have been ordinary, and accompanied at that time with miraculous gifts, as accessory to the strengthening grace of confirmation; it followeth not that the Bishops succeed only to the Apostles in the said ordinary part of their power: because the Apostles being both Bishops and Presbyters, the text maketh not manifest, whether they imposed hands as Presbyters or as Bishops as Durandus[1] saith *Ex illo textu non est clarum an Apostoli confirmaverint tanquam Episcopi vel tanquam sacerdotes: sacri etiam canones hoc clade non determinant.* Augustine[2] saith plainly they did it as Priests. 5. Philip the Evangelist could not do it, and will Bishops presume that they can do more then Philip the Evangelist, the truth is it was an extraordinary and wonderful power exercised by the Apostles.

---

[1] *Durandus in lib. 4. Dist. 7. Quest.* 3
[2] *Quest. veteris et novus testamenti.* 101

Next confirmation belongeth not to the power of jurisdiction, but of order. Bishops and Presbyters are equal in the power of order, as not only many schoolmen of old but also some of our opposites of late do acknowledge. If they will say that they differ only in the exercise of this power; it may be easily answered, that a power granted, and never permitted to be put in execution agreeth not with the wisdom of Christ as Swarez saith, In Aquin part 3, quest. 27, *Si presbyteri ex vi sua ordinationis haberent sufficientum potestalem ordinis ad hoc sacramentum ministrandum sine causa in universum prohiberentur illud conferre.*

Thirdly, they may impose hands in ordination, therefore they may do it also in confirmation. Armacanus reasoneth after this manner out of *1 Timothy 4:14*.

Fourthly, they may minister the Lord's Supper, therefore they may minister it also, for it is not more excellent then the Sacrament of the Supper. Hierome reasoneth after this manner[1].

Fifthly the Sacraments that are for the utility of the people ought not to be reserved, to the Bishop, because it may often fall out that the people depart without this benefit, which they might easily have had at home.

Sixthly, we have the testimony of the ancients. Hierome[2] saith it was the custom in the orient, in Ilyricum, in Italy, in Africa, and in all places in the Apostle's time. Ambrose[3] saith *Apud Egiptum Presbyteri consignant si presens non sit Episcopus.* That the Presbyters consigned, that is, confirmed in Egypt, if the Bishop was not present. Augustine saith the like[4] in the *Decretales*[5] it is said that simple Priests at Constantinople according to the custom, did minister the Sacrament of confirmation. Turrianus reporteth that the Grecians reprove

---

[1] *Epi. ad rusticum Narbonensem*
[2] *Ibid.*
[3] *In Ephes.* 4
[4] *Quest. veteris et novus testamenti.* 101
[5] *Lib.* 1. *tit.* 4. *cap.* 4

the Latins because they inhibit Priests to anoint the foreheads of the baptized with chrisme, as Swarez testified in the place above cited. And the Council of Florence[1] saith *Apud Grecos sacerdotes non Episcopi chrismant.* That the Priests make Chrism: to make Chrism [consecrated oil] is more then to confirm with Chrism. Hierome[2] saith, If the Holy Ghost should come down only at the prayer of the Bishop, these were to be lamented which in prisons, or Castles, or in far places, being baptized by Priests & Deacons, die before the Bishop visit them. The Armenians affirmed that it was lawful to any Priest to confirmed the baptized[3] If Bishops did confirmed in respect of their Episcopal, and not their Priestly consecration, then the Pope cannot dispense in this case and give a simple commission to that effect: but so it is that the Pope hath dispensed in this case. Gregory excuseth himself to Januarius with the custom of his own Kirk for discharging the Priests in the Isle of Sardinia, to confirmed; but he recalled his discharge, when he perceived that offence arose thereupon. Rural Bishops and Abbots did sometime confirm, if we speak regularly; rural Bishops and Abbots were but simple Priests. Hooker[4] confesseth that baptism and confirmation went commonly together. I demand then if the Bishop was present at the baptism of every one within his diocese.

Our opposites are forced to confess, that it is not the proper and essential part of a Bishop's office, but it was given them for honor of their priesthood, according to the saying of Hierome neither was this universal in Hierome's time, for he saith, *Multis in locis id esse tantum factum reperimus ad honorem potiùs sacerdotij quam ob legis necessitatem.* In many places, not all places it was so[5] their honor proved prejudicial to the will

---

[1] *Sess.* 25
[2] *Adversus Lucifer*
[3] *Armaehanus de question. Armanorum. lib.* 11. *cap.* 5
[4] *Eccles. pol. pag.* 353
[5] *Adversus Lucifer*

of the Kirk. Balthasar Lydius saith[1] it was untolerable superstition that the Priest might anoint the breast and the shoulder, but all behooved to abstain from the forehead, except only the Bishop. Beda[2] saith *Confirmatio propter arrogantiam non est concessa singulis sacerdotibus sicut et multa alia.* That for the arrogancy of Bishops, confirmation and many other things were not permitted to Priests. This appropriation of confirmation to Bishops hath made confirmation that is my Lord Bishop's baptism, to be preferred to the Lord's baptism, parents must bring their children to them many miles, as if the Holy Ghost could no where breath but from their fingers. They will scarce once in three years go to them, and so great numbers depart this life without confirmation. They vilipend [neglect] in their deeds, that which they magnify in their words, and the solemn entrance into the society of the communicants which should be made at home in presence of their own congregation, is taken away with their Lordly Bishoping. I end with the saying of Tyndale,[3] "After that Bishops had left preaching then feigned they this dumb ceremony of confirmation, to have somewhat at the least way whereby they might reign over their Diocese. They reserved unto themselves also the christening of bells, and conjuring, or hollowing of Churches and Churchyards and of alters and superalters, and hallowing of chalices, and so forth whatsoever is of honor or profit, which confirmations, and the other conjurations also, they have now committed to their suffragans [bishops]: because they themselves have no leisure to minister such things for their lusts and pleasures and abundance of all things, and for the cumbrance that they have in the King's matters and business of the Realms. One keepeth the privy seal, another the great seal, the third is confessor that is to say a privy traitor and a secret Judas he is president of the Prince his

---

[1] *Notae in disp. Taboritarum. p.* 28
[2] *In psalm* 26
[3] *Obedience pag.* 152

Council, he is an Ambassador; an other sort of the King's secret Council. Woe is unto the Realms, where they are of the Council, As profitable are they verily unto the Realms with their Council, as the wolves unto the sheep, or the foxes unto the geese, thus far." Tyndale.

Of the Administration of the Sacraments in private places

In the ninth head of the first book of discipline, it was thought expedient, that baptism be ministered upon the ordinary days of preaching: not that it is unlawful to baptize whensoever the word is preached: but to remove a gross error wherewith many are deceived, thinking that children be damned if they die without baptism, and to make the people hold the administration of the Sacraments in greater reverence. In the order of baptism set down before the Psalms in meter, it is said, that the Sacraments are not ordained of God to be used in private corners, as charms or sorceries; but left to the Congregation and necessarily annexed to God's word, as seals of the same. In the Assembly holden at Edinburgh *Anno* 1581 in October, it was ordained that the sacraments should not be ministered in private houses, but solemnly, according to the good order hitherto observed, under the pain of deposition, In the confession of faith the cruel judgment against infants departing without the sacrament, and the absolute necessity of baptism are damned. This laudable order hitherto observed, was altered in the late pretended Assembly holden at Perth where was made an act anent the administration of baptism in private houses, when necessity requireth. Item, an act anent the administration, and giving of the holy communion in private houses to sick and infirm persons.

A Sacrament is a public action, to be performed publicly, by public ministers: neither can any necessity or sufficient cause be alleged, wherefore any sacred and public action, should pass in private: Because God's ordinance is to us a Supreme law and necessity, which we ought to obey rather then foster popular ignorance and infirmity. These are Tilenus' words.[1]

The Sacraments were appointed, not only to be signs and seals of invisible graces, but also to be testimonies before the world of our piety and thankfulness towards God, and badges of our profession, distinguishing true Kirks from false. All Sacraments are certain kinds of protestations of our faith saith Aquinas.[2] They ought therefore to be conspicuous and public.

We have spiritual and invisible fellowship and communion with the whole Kirk. Outwardly we profess the same faith and kind of worship, but we do not communicate with the whole Kirk in the public exercises of religion and ministration of the Sacraments, except only mediately in some particular congregation. Visible communion in the holy things of God, is the end of our union and consociation with a particular Kirk. That which we may not attain to in our communion with the whole Kirk militant immediately? We do it mediately in our communion with a particular congregation. This communion ought not to be violate[d].

The minister in ministration of the Sacraments, hath not the only and chief interest, but together with the minister, the Kirk witnessing, consenting, approving, and concurring with prayer and thanksgiving. He is the mouth, but he is not all. The keys of the sacraments are given to the Kirk, howbeit the exercise and dispensation of them be concredited [entrusted] to the pastors.[3] All other actions which concerned the whole Kirk, were done with consent, and in presence of the Kirk: as elections, ordinations, excommunications. By the same reason ought the Sacraments to be ministered with consent, and in presence of the Kirk, seeing they are works of public nature, and public fruit belonging to all.

Sacraments ought to be preserved from contempt, neglect, and corruption. The Sacraments are irreligiously handled,

---

[1] *Syntag. pars. 2. pag. 700*
[2] *Part. 3. quest. 7. act. 5*
[3] *Chrysost. lib. 3. de sacerdotio*

when they are ministered in private places: The Imperial constitution in Justinian[1] dischargeth that holy things be ministered in private houses. Not only are the Sacraments ministered irreligiously in private, brought in contempt, and the public use neglected but also heretics take occasion to corrupt the pure administration of the Sacraments by these privy practices,

The Sacraments are not tied to the material Kirks made of dead stones, but the Kirk made of lively stones. If therefore the congregation be in a wood, a house, or a Cave, the Sacraments may be ministered in a house, a wood or a cave. But then the Sacraments are ministered, not in private but in public because they are ministered in the sight of the whole Congregation.

Christ's promise to be in the midst of two or three convened in his name, cannot be extended to the administration of the Sacraments: for then where two only are convened, the communion might be ministered, and so the private mass defended. Christ reasoneth only from the less to the more. If he will hear the prayers and ratify the censures of two or three, far more of the whole Kirk.

Baptism is a ceremony initiatory of our entrance into the bosom of some visible congregation, or as Calvin saith [2] It is a sacred and solemn introduction into the Kirk of God, and is a testimony of our heavenly burgesship, unto the which those are written up, whom he adopteth to himself, It ought therefore to be public.

Baptism is a sign of Christian profession before the world; it is called therefore the stipulation or interrogation of a good conscience, *1 Peter 3* it ought therefore to be public.

The Congregation should make fruit of the ministration of Baptism, in remembering their own baptism, and the promises made in baptism repeated unto them: it ought

---

[1] *Novel.* 57
[2] *Epist.* 185

therefore to be public, seeing the comfort and benefit in some respects should be common.

Not only the parents, but the Kirk presents the infant before God and concurreth with the minister in prayer for the salvation of the infant, as Tertullian saith, *ut manu facta ambire gratiam pro baptizando possumus*. It ought therefore to be public.

Private baptism hath sprung of the opinion of the necessity of baptism, and doth still foster the same damnable opinion. In the ancient Kirk two solemn times were appointed for baptism, to wit, Pasche and Pentecost, whereby many died without baptism.[1] Many delayed baptism till their latter age. The Clinical baptisms, that is baptisms in the bed were not of that accompt [account] that public baptism had. When the opinion of the necessity of private baptism prevailed, then followed many absurdities, the defense of baptism by women, baptism by a pagan, baptism with puddly water, and disputation whether the mother should be baptized for the safety of the infant in the mother's belly, that is, whether they should be *renati antequam nati*, get the sacrament of the second birth, before they get the first birth.

In private baptism the doctrine of baptism is omitted, for haste to save the soul of the infant, as is thought, and so the Sacrament is not ministered according to the dignity of it: and this hath bred a negligent and careless ministration of baptism in public. The Trullian Synod[2] decreed, that baptism *Nullatenus*, in no case be ministered in a private oratory if it be done otherwise, let the Clergyman be deposed, the likes excommunicate. If in no case, where was then the case of necessity?

Private baptism hath bred a new kind of baptism, that is, a baptism by supposition. For if the child baptized in private convalesce they baptize it over again, in case they doubt it was baptized in a right form, saying, If thou be not baptized,

---

[1] *Socrat. lib.* 5. *cap.* 21
[2] Can. 59

& I baptize thee in the name of the Father, &c. What if the childe was already baptized? Is not the public baptism rebaptization? But the decree of Alexander the third is warrant sufficient for this conditional baptism.

Baptism was solemn in the primitive Kirk, as we may read of John baptized in Jordan, and Christ's Disciples baptizing, and the new Converts in the Acts: some were not baptized in any visible Kirk, because they had not the occasion, as the Eunuch, and the Centurion. No man will deny but in the infancy of a Kirk, a private baptism may be tolerated: but we speak of a Kirk constituted. When the Kirk of God was in families, no wonder that circumcision was ministered in families: but after that the Kirk was constituted among God's people, the ministration of circumcision was public, and is at this day ministered in the Synagogue, where a Synagogue is to be had. The Lord appointed a precise day for circumcision, which might not be prevented. It was no wonder therefore if they had not ever opportunity of a solemn convention. There is no precise day set down for baptism. The mark of circumcision howbeit secret, was permanent, and easily tried, baptism is not so. The Kirk therefore ought to be assured of the baptism of such as are reputed fellow-heirs with whom they must have the communion of Saints and visible communion of holy exercises. As any particular member is cut off from their fellowship by excommunication with consent, and in the presence of the Kirk, *1 Corinthians 5:4,5* so ought every particular member be received in their fellowship with their knowledge and consent convened together.

The Lord's Supper ought to be public, we have a spiritual union with the whole Kirk; but because it is not possible to celebrate a sacramental communion with the whole Kirk militant, the Lord hath appointed us to celebrate a sacramental communion with some particular Kirk. We that are many, are one bread, and one body, because we are partakers of one bread, *1 Corinthians 10:17*. We cannot then be one body sacramentally, except we be partakers of one bread.

Other feasts may be private in private houses, but the Lord's Supper ought to be public, 1 *Corinthians 11:12*. When ye convene to eat, tarry one for another, 1 *Corinthians 11:33*. *Synaxis* a word signifying as much as Synagogue, was one of the names given of old to this sacrament.

This sacrament is a bond of love, a sinew of public assemblies, a badge of our public profession. The Kirk's interest, the dignity of the sacrament, and other general reasons before mentioned, may be applied in particular to this sacrament, to prove that the ministration thereof ought to be public.

The communion was sent to the sick in the time, or immediately after the action in Justin Martyr his time. It became afterward to be reserved for the use of dying persons. Augustine who misconstrued *John 3:5* for the necessity of baptism, did also misconstrue the words of *John 6*. Except a man eat the flesh, &c. for the necessity of the Eucharist. This erroneous opinion of the necessity of the Eucharist, made the ancients to give it not only to aged persons departing this life for their *Victucum*, that is, their voyage victuals, but also to infants and babes, and that for the space of six hundred years: yea some put the Eucharist into the mouths of the dead, lest they should want their voyage victual. Such horrible profanations of the holy Sacrament proceeded of this opinion of necessity: and yet in all antiquity we read not that the communion was celebrated at the sick man's bedside. The consecrated bread was only sent to him.

Clinical communions have not only bred, and still do foster the opinion of absolute necessity, but also of *opus operatum*, of a preposterous confidence in the last voyage victual, of coldness in the public service of God, when we are in health, of distrust of our salvation, if we want it at that time. Calvin saith,[1] *Difficillimum est hic cavere ne alios superstitio, alios ambitio & vana ostentatio ad petendum sollicitet.*

---

[1] *Epist.* 361

They say the sick should not be left destitute of comfort. This reason ariseth of the opinion of necessity, as if there were no other means to comfort the sick, or as if the comfort of the public communion endured only for the present time, and not for the time to come. There is a fair occasion offered, *James* 5 of private communion, and yet there is no mention made of it in that place. If the vow, and desire of baptism may supply the want of baptism, then may also the vow and desire of the Eucharist do the like; seeing the Rhemists[1] acknowledge, that they do eat the flesh and drink the blood of Christ, which join in heart, and desire, with the partakers of the Sacrament. To communicate spiritually and mystically, is necessary, but not sacramentally, when it cannot be done conveniently, and without breach of order.

Some Divines condescend thus far, that the communion may be sent to the sick in the time of the public action. But Tilenus saith,[2] Whatsoever necessity be pretended, scarce any sufficient cause can be rendered, wherefore the public action should pass in private, because the ordinance of God is of supreme necessity. The comforts of the infirm ministered out of order, doth rather foster the public infirmity of the Kirk, then heal the private infirmity of the sick.

FINIS

---

[1] *On* John 6. sect. 8
[2] *Syntag. part.* 2. *pag.* 722

CPSIA information can be obtained at www.ICGtesting.com
Printed in the USA
LVOW06s1649220614

391093LV00003B/31/P